A. Egmont Hake

Regeneration : a reply to Max Nordau

A. Egmont Hake

Regeneration : a reply to Max Nordau

ISBN/EAN: 9783744657396

Printed in Europe, USA, Canada, Australia, Japan

Cover: Foto ©ninafisch / pixelio.de

More available books at **www.hansebooks.com**

REGENERATION

A REPLY TO

MAX NORDAU

WESTMINSTER
ARCHIBALD CONSTABLE
& CO 1895

CONTENTS

CHAPTER I
WHO IS THE CRITIC? 1

CHAPTER II
DUSK OR DAWN! 27

CHAPTER III
MYSTICISM AND THE UNKNOWABLE 44

CHAPTER IV
THE BANKRUPTCY OF SCIENCE 74

CHAPTER V
SYMBOLISM AND LOGIC 96

CHAPTER VI
THE LIGHT OF RUSSIA 111

CHAPTER VII
THE REAL IBSEN 136

CHAPTER VIII
RICHARD WAGNER 188

CONTENTS

CHAPTER IX
THE RELIGION OF SELF 236

CHAPTER X
AN ETHICAL INQUISITION 247

CHAPTER XI
VIGOROUS AFFIRMATIONS 265

CHAPTER XII
REGENERATION 298

REGENERATION

CHAPTER I

WHO IS THE CRITIC?

VOLTAIRE said that if all the celestial bodies are inhabited, our earth must be the madhouse of the universe. To us who know the era of the great cynic only as recorded by the history of Dryasdusts, and the flippant memoirs and autobiographies of his contemporaries, his biting sarcasm cannot be considered undeserved. But, with regard to our own times, most of us would probably hesitate to brand our present state of culture, our modern civilization, as a fool's paradise.

It is a truism that an historical epoch can only be correctly studied at a distance in time, as the outlines of a mountain can only be studied at a distance in space. The actor in a piece, though intimately acquainted with his own part and the accessories with which he comes in contact, cannot form a just idea of the impression which the play, with its more or less successful rendering, its scenery, and other spectacular effects, produces on the mind of the average spectator. A super who is ignorant of stage management and of the precise results the manager aims at might deem many things going on behind the stage both foolish and ridiculous. To him the frantic efforts of some actor, or scene-shifter, to produce some ordinary effect might well appear as lunacy.

The judgment we form concerning the time we live in runs a great risk of being biassed by the narrowness of the vista we can command. The interdependence of causes simultaneously at work, the co-operation of impulses active at a great distance, the peculiarities of circumstances surrounding each leading phenomenon, the real intentions of leading characters, secret motives in groups and parties—all this represents so many sealed books to the contemporary to be gradually opened only by future historians.

There are no doubt many facilities ready to hand for the man who in modern times desires to study his own epoch, which were not available in the past. Distances are practically suppressed, the whole of civilized humanity has been placed in intimate connection, a highly developed Press records daily events everywhere in a minute fashion, to the making of books there is no end, and in every direction an elaborate mechanism is established for the obtaining of rapid and precise information. In fact, the Kammergelehrte, who, like Kant, would study the world-phenomenon without leaving his native town, would in our days stand a better chance of obtaining completer and exacter information than any philosopher before him.

But, despite the quasi-ubiquitousness the modern philosopher enjoys, he would indulge in self-deception were he tempted to believe that he had secured all the data requisite to judge the contemporaries of his race as they act, live, feel, and think during the closing years of this century.

For, against the easy access to information, must be placed the mass of intricate problems that arise with every step of progress, the multitude of ideas which strive for realization, the bewilderment which ensues on crumbling systems and religions, new discoveries, new theories, new and complicated associations of ideas, new and hazy aspirations, sympathies, and yearnings—for all of which words cannot be coined fast enough. Every day we witness political, social, economic, and psychological phenomena, the explanation of which would demand not only an enormous amount of knowledge, but reasoning powers and a freedom from bias seldom blended in one human mind. Facts, circumstances, theories, human actions, and human ideas, change and intermingle so constantly and so rapidly as to produce bewilderment capable of misleading any philosopher who attempts to gauge them with the instruments of the past and in conformity with the doctrines of the school to which he belongs.

What renders it still more difficult to appraise any epoch, and especially the present one, is the intimate interdependence of all the phenomena to be observed. The idiosyncrasies of a sovereign, or of a minister, influence legislation, legislation influences public institutions, public institutions influence the upper classes, and the upper classes influence the masses. But legislation, institutions, the upper classes and the people are influenced from a great number of other directions, while they again influence the sovereign and the minister. Thus it would be impossible to attribute with accuracy a given number of effects to special causes: for every cause is the effect of another cause, and every effect produces other effects. For instance, art and literature may strongly influence men in power as well as the masses, while no one will deny that men in power, as well as the political and social condition of the masses, exercise a strong influence on art and literature. And then, on the top of it all, —as if worse to confound the confusion of the man with a system, trivial incidents intervene and bring about a new series of causes and effects evidently destined to operate as long as humanity lasts. So interdependent are the actors in the human drama, so complete is the intricate and sensitive mechanism of causes and effects, and so overcharged with energy are the social dynamos, that any fool, any child, any trivial accident, may move one of the countless points arranged by circumstances, and thus hurl the engine of events in new and dangerous directions.

These, and many other difficulties, encountered by the student of his own time are largely responsible for his opinions, often savouring as much of his idiosyncrasy, his professional and national prejudices as of an independent inquiry. In order to choose between the maze of highways and by-ways, in order to judge whether he be moving forwards, backwards, or in a circle, he gropes for some kind of a compass and naturally clutches at that which his idiosyncrasy proffers. When we therefore meet with an appraiser of his own epoch, it behoves us to bear in mind the standpoint from which he has contemplated the world-phenonemon, and with what bias and prejudice his views have been coloured. The old Greek story of the sandal-maker, who became prejudiced against a work of art because the artist had made a mistake in the arrangement of the sandal-strings, points its moral. The prejudices arising from trade, personal interests, and many other palpable sources are not difficult to trace and to evade, but where is the man whose views have not been influenced by his nationality, his religion, his favourite science or art, his love, his hatred, or his ambition?

It is to such influences, often considered by the influenced as so many advantages and seldom sufficiently noticed by his critics, that we often owe the apparent profundity and exhaustiveness of an appreciation which in reality is one-sided.

Education, and, still more, an intense study of one special branch of knowledge, rich in important and striking results, naturally tend to strengthen the student's faith and his belief in the capabilities of his favourite science. The brain-cells, influenced by the will, and habitually becoming stimulated by presentations—emanating from the subject on which the student has concentrated his attention—adapt themselves gradually to the perception of such presentations, and by re-acting on other cells render the whole organism disposed to seek such presentations. In plain language, the specialist in one science has a great aptitude for discovering such causes and such effects as his favourite science has best elucidated, while he is tempted to overlook other causes and other effects which may be of equal or greater importance.

The specialist attains to a mastery of his own subject, and often acquires a strong bias regarding other subjects, because he pursues his inquiries somewhat after the same fashion as the dog follows the scent of the game. By training, the dog is familiar with the smell of the animal pursued, and, bent on following the trail, he pays no attention to any other scents or smells that he encounters in his course. In the same way the specialist rapidly perceives and minutely studies any phenomena, however slight, with which his favourite science has rendered him familiar, while he is apt to disregard phenomena demanding fresh studies and threatening to be inexplicable by investigation confined to the lines which he prefers to follow.

Thus, if a law-student were to write a treatise on our epoch, he would endeavour to show that the jurisprudence, the law, and the courts—in fact, the whole legal mechanism—is the most important feature in our civilization, and that on which progress or retrogression most depends. As remedies for our evils, he would propose simpler, or more complicated forms of procedure, more or less enactments, according to his own idiosyncrasies.

A military man would consider a development on military lines as true progress. He would yearn to draft the whole nation into the army! He would favour universal conscription, as Lord Wolseley does, and might, like Count Moltke, look upon war as a healthy bracing, an epuration, of a race, and as an indispensable corrective to over-population. He would cite the expansion of the chest in Germany as a proof of the power of military training to further physical development, and would look upon strict military discipline as the means of establishing moral order in a country.

A theologian would point to the immense influence exercised by Christianity upon humanity, and would insist upon the religious aspect of every question, and, like Mr. Drummond, would see in every new discovery a confirmation of his peculiar dogmas. His remedy would be more ritualism, or more liberal doctrines, or more emotion in religion, according to his High Church, Broad Church, or Low Church creed.

Philosophical religionists, like Mr. Benjamin Kidd and others who pin their faith to the development of the altruistic feeling in human beings, would endeavour to reconcile all phenomena under their observation with their theory of social evolution.

If therefore we wish to form a correct judgment of our own time and our own contemporaries, we must not allow ourselves to be guided exclusively by a scientist of one specialty. We ought to be all the more on our guard, as the great erudition and the profound study which each modern specialist has brought to bear on his subject gives to his theories a striking plausibility, a savour of exact science to such an extent as to sway our opinions in favour of the latest treatise we have read.

Politicians, sociologists, economists, biologists, theologians and the æsthetes have had their say and have each in their turn exercised a periodical spell over the public mind. It is now the turn of the alienists. Dr. Max Nordau has by his book entitled "Degeneration" produced no small sensation throughout the world, and not least in this country. Though his work may not have made the stir of a sensational novel read by the millions, there can be little doubt that it has imposed itself on every educated mind in the country. It is no exaggeration to say that, like a sharp trumpet-blast, it has awakened the educated classes from the lethargy consequent upon the din of clashing opinions and contradictory systems. This volume has once more roused us to the fact that we, as individuals, as a nation, as a race, are travelling at comet-speed towards a goal of which we have no inkling. It sternly suggests that we are on the wrong road and that a fate of a most horrible description is rapidly befalling us—an affliction in most people's view worse that annihilation. Madness is shown to be insidiously invading our minds, and by its contagious nature threatening to prove Voltaire's biting sarcasm a stern prophecy.

It is no wonder that his work has become as it were a nightmare to millions of minds. If its diagnosis and its conclusions are as irrefutable as to most people they appear to be, we indeed live in a fool's paradise : our leaders, our authorities, our men of genius, are not the beacons we have held them to be, but will-o'-the-wisps luring us into the bottomless quagmires of lunacy ; the progression we vaunted is a slippery plane sliding us back to bestiality ; our means for raising the masses are so many slashes at the bonds of moral order and decency, calculated to unloose the brutish Loke of modern democracy ; unbridled animal appetites threaten to take the place of law and religion ; all social order is being undermined ; and the vilest instincts press for gratification in lust, rapine, and murder. With all the solemnity, moral persuasiveness, and scientific authority of a medical practitioner, Max Nordau tells us that a mortal disease is invading our race, and that with the end of the century the "dusk" of humanity begins.

Before we accept the views of Max Nordau, before we have recourse to the drastic remedies he seems to recommend, it is right that we should subject his theories to the closest investigation. If his work were one of exact science, there would be no necessity to refer to the personality of the author, to his peculiar point of view, and to his predilections. But, as his work partakes largely of the nature of special pleading, as his methods of reasoning are those of the enthusiastic specialist, and as his postulates are strongly coloured by racial, national, and professional bias, the more we know of him the more easily shall we follow him in his progress on the highways of logic and in his deviations from them. Human language is not so perfect as to allow us to dispense with the additional light on expressed ideas which may be derived from one's knowledge of the speaker who gives utterance to them. To study the author as well as his work is all the more permissible, as this volume is not intended as a complete refutation of Max Nordau's conclusions, but rather aims at separating the dross from the gold and at giving him, as well as his work, their right place and their true value as telling factors in the development of our race. Indeed, this is exactly the method adopted by Max Nordau in his study, not to say dissection, of his contemporaries.

It must be clearly understood however that there is no intention of going to the length to which Max Nordau has gone in speaking of men of the day—an abuse of literature which recalls the literary squabbles of past generations. The gross vituperation and the coarse calumny he levels against those he denounces will certainly not enhance his popularity or inspire confidence in his methods in England. In fact, his frequent indulgence in personalities would have prejudiced his work enormously were it not for the overwhelming testimony it offers of the fact that its author's mind is conspicuously devoid of the sense of the ridiculous. Had it not been for this peculiar mental defect, his treatment of his opponents could not have failed to remind him of the disputing doctors in Molière's "Malade Imaginaire."

Here we have to do not with the man, but with the author,—not with his relations to his private surroundings, but with his relation to the presentations he receives, the ideas he elaborates, and the conclusions he proclaims.

In "Degeneration," Max Nordau evidently strives to take a cosmopolitan standpoint. Only in three or four places does he speak of Germany as his own country, while he displays a remarkable erudition in foreign literature, but only a superficial knowledge of foreign circumstances. Unconsciously however he constantly betrays his German nationality. To say that he is a typical German involves by no means any slur upon his views, has nothing to do with the fact that the Germans are at this moment —for reasons entirely independent of German worth —rather unpopular in this country. It is his book that clearly announces him as a German, just as the books of Drummond and Benjamin Kidd announce them to be English. In other words, his methods, his views, his predispositions, his standards, his ideals are thoroughly German.

Few countries have so strong a power of inspiring love for their institutions and their characteristics as Germany. Not only is the German spell over those who are born and bred in the country, but foreigners who reside there any length of time generally become thoroughly Germanized. Even English people, whose characteristic it is to create a little England around them wherever they go, are remarkably susceptible to German influence when living in the country.

Despite the propensity of many Germans, complained of by Max Nordau in his book, to imitate French art and literature, the German people have strongly pronounced characteristics, opinions, feelings, and views. We, here in England, have ample opportunity of observing the tenacity of the German bias. We sometimes meet with Germans who have conquered their native propensities and thoroughly assimilated themselves with the English nation. But, on the other hand, many Germans, when settled among us, continue to look on everything through German spectacles, and utterly fail to grasp, or even superficially to understand, the English spirit. This refers, of course, only to those who are actually born in Germany. The second generation is invariably more English than the English. We often meet with Teutons who have come young to England, gained a position here, married English wives, brought up a large family of English children, and who yet remain as German as any *Spiesbürger* in Berlin. They do not appear so to the casual observer. Their business relations, their acquaintances, their wives, and their children, being all English, expect them to be English. They therefore assume an English outward garb, but as soon as circumstances allow them to drop their English character the German characteristics of these " tame Englishmen " come out as strong as ever. These facts are elicited in no critical spirit, but simply as proofs of the tenacity of the German bias.

The practical result of this bias is an open or secret contempt for English views, a distrust in English institutions, a want of sympathy with the English race, and doubts about the future of the British Empire.

If we wish Max Nordau's nationality to throw light on the working of his mind, we must realize what are the most essential traits of the average German.

Not yet completely freed from feudal institutions, it is natural that the German people should associate moral and political order, good administration, and personal protection, with feudal institutions. Hence an immense respect for those in authority and a contempt for the masses, even on the part of the masses. Democratic government and individual liberty inspire the German with great distrust, because he considers that the introduction into Germany of such features would mean a social upheaval in which the meagre advantages which now each individual enjoys might be lost.

As in Germany all initiative belongs to the authorities, the people have become accustomed to bend to superiors, and where an Englishman would attempt to establish a Free Order, the Germans can conceive nought but discipline. A great number of enlightened Germans submit tacitly to all kinds of authorities because they are morally convinced that this is best for themselves and their country; but a large part of the masses, having always found that the authorities gain their ends by the use of police and military force, submit only because they are obliged. Hence a deep-rooted feeling of discontent in a nation constantly compelled to do the bidding of others. This discontent has engendered a hatred against the upper classes similar to that which in France paved the way for the first Revolution. The fear of the outbreak of this hatred gives, in the eyes of the German middle-class, an extra halo to authority.

The love of following authorities, instead of standing alone, is in Germany not confined to the domain of politics. While Englishmen, down to the wage-earning labourer, have, or believe they have, their own opinions about politics, administration, religion, social affairs, and even scientific problems, the Germans have an accepted authority in each of these branches. Were we to question, say, a hundred Germans in a Bierhalle, or any other public place, as to their opinions on the above-named subjects, the replies would be simply an enumeration of their authorities in each branch of knowledge. Though this characteristic is a misfortune to Germany, to the Germans it savours of a quaint reasonableness. A German socialist, asked why he blindly accepted Liebknecht's views, replied, "I should be both silly and conceited if I, a scantily educated man, with no leisure and means for study, could believe myself capable of forming a better opinion than Herr Liebknecht, who has brought a remarkable mind and great knowledge to bear on political questions."

This reasoned self-depreciation, this blind faith in authorities, accounts for much in Germany which would be impossible in England. The way, for example, in which the youths of the country are forced into the ranks of the army against their will and inclination would be out of the question with us. Here, the great majority of young men would simply refuse, and to coerce them by military executions would involve a wholesale slaughter against which the whole nation would revolt. There have been young men in Germany who, on principle, have resisted the compulsory service, but brutal punishment has quickly dissuaded those of their comrades who secretly admired them from following their example. Nothing could be more unjust to the German people than to attribute to cowardice this lamb like submission. German youths are as brave as those of any other nation, and what to us English might appear a want of both moral and physical courage is simply the powerful influence of the German bias.

Enough has been said to show that German education and German surroundings tend to foster in the human mind veneration for authority and aristocracy, contempt for the plebeian, distrust of liberty, a firm belief in the unquenchable power of man's lowest instincts, a nervous demand for authoritative repression of human passions, contentment with a prosaic existence, small resources, and poor prospects.

It is natural that a nation, whose mind is moulded in such a form, should despair of the practical realization of its ideals; that the aspirations of the German race for liberty, enjoyment, and romance should seek an outlet in the realms of the imagination; and that the Germans should be a sentimental race. In this they differ diametrically from our nation. The young German, when his humdrum work-day is over, will plunge into books of poetry, romance and adventure. He will worship and eagerly follow his pet heroes, but to emulate them in practical life, as a rule, does not occur to him.

His romantic admiration of female beauty, and his sentiment of love, have nothing to do with his marriage. He postpones, as a rule, the taking to himself a wife until he is fairly successful in life, when pure romantic love has ceased to exercise any spell over him, and he expects that his marriage should improve his social position and procure him a circle of desirable friends. His poetical notions of love do not interfere with the choice of a wife. What he looks for is a young woman with practical qualities, likely to be a useful *Hausfrau*, and when he has found her, he loses no time in suppressing all her poetical notions and soon reduces her to a submissive drudge.

No suspicion of inconsistency enters the mind of an average German when he reads or writes romances of love and chivalry in which the hero shows the most refined courtesy, commits deeds of self-abnegation and daring in honour of his lady-love, and exercises the utmost tact in shielding her from every harsh and unpleasant impression, and at the same time treats his wife as one devoid of all claims upon his consideration. He will exact from her such small menial services as the slave performs for his master. He will expect her to work constantly for him, the family, and the house. He will not allow her enough time or money for her toilet, for pleasure, for book, and social intercourse. He will not stir to save her trouble or fatigue. He will come to the table in dressing-gown and slippers, and coolly look for special dishes for himself, while his wife and children have to content themselves with cheap garbage.

Germans of the middle-class who come to England frequently express their amazement at the way in which English husbands constantly pay attention to their wives. They call it undignified for the bread-winner and master of the house, on return from a day of professional work, to "dance attendance" on his wife, whose duty it is to serve her husband.

The German, prior to marriage, allows his poetical notions to be disturbed as little by his sexual emotions as by his marriage plans. In a methodical and business-like way he gratifies the former in police-supervised establishments, and what he looks upon as "constitutional sprees" are never allowed to interfere with the course of his affairs. After a night of debauch he will turn up in his studio, his office, or his home, smiling and happy as if nothing had happened.

We record these observations with no desire to criticise or to underrate the German character. Nor do we wish to insinuate that hypocrisy and profligacy are non-existent in England. We simply wish to show that the development of the German race has induced them to conceive ideals entirely unrealizable, and to dream of aims so far off in time as to render them unattainable.

It will be evident to all who have read "Degeneration" that Max Nordau is under the influence of a strong German bias. As we proceed, we shall have occasion to point out how in many instances this bias has warped his perceptions, his reasoning, and his conclusions.

From characteristics revealed in his work, the observant reader will, no doubt, conclude that Max Nordau belongs to the Jewish race. The view he takes of the disgraceful Jew-baiting tendencies now prevailing in Germany is based on exactly the same mistakes committed by the Jews themselves, as we shall have an opportunity of verifying later on. He is evidently a free-thinking Jew, a type which we meet with everywhere, and against which as few objections can be raised as against any other type of man. The free-thinking Jew is generally clever, well-instructed, moral, and cheerful. His good qualities however do not prevent him from having his peculiar characteristics, which naturally influence his perceptions and his feelings. He has generally a cut-and-dried life-philosophy based on science and common-sense as well as on Jewish authorities. He distrusts democracy, especially Christian democracy, and feels never quite safe except under laws and institutions which allow him to assume such ascendancy as his mental qualifications can secure for him, and those who think with him. He does not seek for primary causes, and sets up no spiritual ideals. Though he may not be religious, he has yet retained something of the monotheist creed, the predilection for worldly affairs, and the habit of looking forward to a future life rather in his descendants than in a heaven—a view which always characterized his race. His philosophy is nothing if not practical. His aims are immediate, and, as a rule, he eagerly embraces all the teachings of the materialist scientists.

Max Nordau is a modern scientist. He is not a pioneer in science, but a most persevering and plodding student of the works of others. He belongs to that class of *savants* who spend almost all their time and all their energy in reading up the authorities. So vast an erudition as he has acquired cannot be attained to without some sacrifice in other directions. The constant absorption of other peoples' opinions and theories compels the judgment to lean more and more on authorities, and this unfits it, to some extent, for independent action. It is the indefatigable readers who most blindly follow authorities, and it suffices to glance at Max Nordau's dedication to

Professor Lombroso to understand to what an extent he is subject to the influence of "Masters."

The pride taken by a scientist in his science, and the great practical results achieved by scientific investigations, naturally tend to foster an implicit confidence in its tenets. This has been especially the case during the last decades, so remarkable for religious tolerance. As the faith in old dogmas has receded, science has advanced, and in many cases taken its place. That such has been the case has naturally flattered the votaries of science, and tempted them to become prophets as well as investigators. They have come to look upon systems as dogmas, speculations as absolute truths, and in this fashion scientific superstition tends to take the place of religious superstition.

The scientifically superstitious man is an example of the dangers of a little knowledge. Not that our men of science, including the superstitious scientists, are defective in such knowledge as is attainable at our present stage, but the sum total of all human knowledge is still, and is probably destined ever to be, only partial and extremely superficial. Compared with the knowledge in the past, modern science represents an immense progress, but as to throwing light on the great secret of the Universe, far from having done anything of the sort, it has, on the contrary, revealed more and more inexplicable wonders, and placed us face to face with more insoluble problems. Though trite, the aphorism that the more we learn the more we realize our ignorance is truer to-day than ever. It is natural and excusable that devotees of a science which to them has revealed wonderful results should raise abnormal expectations with regard to its future possibilities, and also that vanity, a weakness often co-existent with vast knowledge, should prompt a scientist to extol and glorify science far beyond the bounds of reason ; for any worship offered to science rebounds necessarily on its high priests. This impossibility to realize the limits in which science moves, and the yearning for admiration, lie at the base of scientific superstition.

The scientifically superstitious man believes that science has adequately replied to those great questions which humanity has been asking itself for the last five thousand years. How was creation originated? For what purpose did it come into existence? What is man? What does the scheme of humanity involve? Have we existed before our birth? Shall we live after death? What is the origin of evil? What is eternity? What is boundlessness in space? What is reason? What is instinct? and so on.

If his excessive study has not seriously impaired his independent reasoning powers, the superstitious scientist may confess that these questions have not been replied to by science, but there will still lurk in his mind the belief that one day science will answer them.

He does not distinguish between nomenclature, registration, and classification on the one hand, and explanation on the other. When he has named any newly-discovered substance, force, or phenomenon, he imagines that he has explained them. He believes that he has accounted for what is called matter when he has evolved the atom, and that he has unveiled the secret of life when he has discovered the protoplasm or the cell.

All scientists are not affected by scientific superstition. They generally suffer from it in an inverse ratio to the actual knowledge they have acquired. The pioneer in science generally exhibits less of this weakness than those who simply act as commentators and elaborators of other men's discoveries.

The votaries of certain sciences are less apt to indulge in scientific superstition than those of other branches. Thus, astronomers rarely exhibit any such symptoms, while biologists are more apt to do so, and psychologists are more scientifically superstitious than any other class of scientists. It might be hazardous to attempt an explanation of this fact, but may it not be found in the obviousness of outward infinity, and the impalpability of inward infinity?

Later on we shall have ample occasion to show

to what an extent Max Nordau's mind has been clouded by scientific superstition.

Finally, it must be pointed out that Max Nordau is an enemy to France. It is only human in any German. The stupendous armament of France is ostentatiously promoted with the object of revenge upon Germany. France, in her sulks over the lost provinces, takes every opportunity of showing animosity, and this despite the conciliatory attitude of her Government.

Though nearly a quarter of a century has elapsed since the disastrous war between Germany and France, the bad feeling between the two nations has unfortunately been kept up. France cannot forget the loss of her provinces, and, though the attitude of the French Government is conciliatory, outbursts of a feeling of hatred against Germany, accompanied by provocative language on the part of irresponsible men, constantly occur.

The German people, with a vivid recollection of the French invasion early in the century, and perhaps taking the expressions of the war-party in France too seriously, look upon the French nation as their arch-enemies. By the celebration of anniversaries painful to the French, and other means, the German Government keeps the animosity between the two nations alive, and impresses the people with the opinion that the heavy taxes it has to pay for armaments are made indispensable by the enmity of France. It is, therefore, natural that hatred against France should prevail in Germany.

We understand that Max Nordau for a considerable time was the Paris correspondent of German papers, and we may take for granted that he would not have been able to please his German readers had he not been strongly biassed in favour of Germany against France—a fact to which his work bears ample witness.

Such is, then, the man who, in his undaunted faith in his science and in himself, in the name of truth and the welfare of humanity, and undeterred by the penalties of the Great Council and Hell Fire, has said to his brethren, — to the one, "You are Raca!" and to the other, "Thou fool!"

CHAPTER II

DUSK OR DAWN!

MAX NORDAU'S theory is that the educated classes of the world are degenerating; that the peculiarities in passions, tastes, pastimes, and moods, bear witness to such degeneration; that the cause must be found in the physical condition of the brains of such authors and artists as for the time being have the ear and the eye of the public; that the remedy against degeneration may be found in a moral quasi-compulsory supervision on the part of the non-degenerate over degenerate authors and artists. If we are not entirely exact in this summary of his postulates and conclusions, it is to a great extent Max Nordau's fault, because nowhere does he give any decided statement of the scope of his book.

In his first chapter he goes out of his way in order to protest against the misconception which represents him as having insinuated that the whole of humanity exhibited signs of decay, and he declares that his remarks apply exclusively to the educated classes. Were this absolutely true, there would have been but small occasion for his remarkable work. But over and over again in the pages of "Degeneration" he speaks of the masses as partly affected by degeneration, and of the danger of the contamination spreading from the educated classes to the masses. He mentions the extreme Socialists and the Anarchists as the victims of the mental disease he investigates. And yet he flatters himself that the proletariat is not as the upper classes are, and bases his opinion on the fact that they appear satisfied with the old forms of art and poetry, that they prefer George Ohnet's novels to the works of the symbolists, and Mascagni's music to that of Wagner.

These statements evidently emanate from one who has mingled little with the people. The truth is that the newest books, the newest music, the newest pictures, only slowly reach the working classes, and when such works are the outcome of temporary fashion and mood, they might not reach them at all. But this by no means proves that the working classes do not experience the impulses which prompt the predilections of the upper classes.

If Max Nordau's views of the proletariat in general were confirmed by actualities prevailing among the German proletariat, a heavy load would be lifted from the shoulders of the German Government. But, judging from the German Press—the official Press as well as the Socialistic—or from the speeches of so high an authority as the Emperor himself, there exists but little of the Philistine contentment with the present order of things of which the author speaks. On the contrary, the Emperor complains that the discontented working classes are losing their respect for things that used to be sacred to them, such as patriotism, feudal loyalty, religion, etc.

Does Max Nordau mean to tell us that the pornographic novels of certain French authors, that the works of Émile Zola and other realists, are not read by the masses in France? Who then pays for the enormous editions issued after millions have read them in *feuilleton*? Or does he wish us to believe that only the aristocracy and the upper classes in France have been affected by the mysticism which finds its outlet in the pilgrimage to Lourdes?

As to the working classes in the English-speaking countries, which, by the way, signify so little to Max Nordau that he not even once mentions them in his work, are they not children of their time, and do they not reflect every tendency, every virtue, and every vice in the upper classes? Not only would Max Nordau find, were he to investigate the matter, that those stigmata of degeneration which he refers to as such—Individualism and Anarchism—are making big strides among the English-speaking working classes, but that the taste for criminal and realistic literature is growing in popularity. He would even find Wagner's music intensely applauded by audiences recruited from the working class.

Far from developing ethically in different directions, the upper and the lower classes in this country move together, each simultaneously influencing the other. While the lower classes follow the upper classes in many things—for example, politics, dress, etc.—the upper classes obtain their comic songs, their humorous stories, and most of their fun from the lower classes.

The impartial observer cannot fail to notice the kinship which exists between the proclivities of the two extremes of English society—the wealthiest nobility and the poorest labourers. Both these classes are intensely fond of sports, both degrade sport by betting, both are given to lavish expenditure, both pride themselves on physical force and pluck above everything. Both are prone to disregard the sanctity of marriage. Both indulge freely in the pleasures of eating and drinking. Individuals of both classes get on together better than they do with the middle classes. And both are only superficially religious.

Perhaps this remarkable community of tastes and

views may account for what has always been an inexplicable enigma to foreigners,—the conservative working man.

Max Nordau classes, among the indications of decay, the yearning for freedom from outward control and for complete personal independence. It is true he takes for granted that such yearnings for individual liberty aim at the realization of bestial propensities now, according to him, kept in check only by law, police, and public opinion. We shall, later on, find that he has completely misunderstood the attempts to shake off all shackles which he has noticed. Here it suffices to point out that the longing for individual freedom, which manifests itself in a thousand ways unobserved by Max Nordau, and in the upper classes takes the shape of a revolt against conventionality, is conspicuous among the working classes of Great Britain. This year's elections have proved beyond doubt that the tendency towards State Socialism which characterized the Liberal policy is fast becoming distasteful to the rank and file of voters. The tyranny, which, in the name of Socialism was exercised by the Trades Unions, will soon be a thing of the past. When at its height of development the Trades Unions hardly comprised one-fifth of the working classes, and now already the movement is in full retrogression. The Free Labour Association, though only lately called into existence, meets with increasing support, and may no doubt be looked upon as an expression of our working classes' new-born love of freedom.

This change of mind, or, as Max Nordau would call it, this degeneration, also accounts for the present halt in the advance of the Socialistic propaganda and the rapid spread of moderate but decisive Anarchist opinions which in no small degree contributed to the recent Conservative victory at the polls.

What is here stated regarding the British working classes is true regarding the working classes of all the English-speaking countries. Everywhere we find a strong yearning for freedom from control. The remarkable point about the expressions of this yearning is that, though the votaries of the revolt against State tyranny have so far not been able to formulate any complete or practical scheme for the life of a State, or community, governed by the best instincts of the human being instead of by law, their views are rapidly gaining ground. This is especially the case in the United States, where Mr. Tucker, the editor of a little journal called *Liberty*, is steadily extending his influence.

The author of "Degeneration" distorts reality when he supposes that the upper classes of a country can be corrupt and degenerate, while the masses conform to that German Philistine ideal—a very poor one indeed—which Max Nordau would fain hold up to them. This is proved by the fact that it is in their relations with the masses that the corruption of the upper classes becomes conspicuous, and that only through response from the masses can many forms of such corruptions become possible.

It would take us too far to record all the proofs that actualities furnish of this fact. We shall simply point out one of the many conditions in the masses which promote corruption in the educated classes, namely, poverty. The appalling, demoralizing, brutalising poverty in the large modern cities,—this poisonous fungus grown out of modern government and political corruptions, not only kills the sense of self-respect and decency in its victims, but renders prostitution, through sheer hunger and suffering, the trade of millions. It is poverty among the masses which undermines the artistic feeling of the nation, stands in the way of applied art, and compels the caterer of popular amusements to appeal to low passions and brutal instincts. Our epoch is not the first example in history where masses of destitute people exercise all their ingenuity in corrupting the wealthy citizens in the hope of snatching some crumbs of their wealth.

Dire poverty it is, with its hovels, its rags, and its diseases, which gives riches their immense value in the eyes of the people. It creates a thirst for gold.

No man thinks himself safe from falling into the abyss of modern poverty until he has amassed a large fortune and placed himself in the position of amassing more. The love of wealth corrupts Literature, Art, the Press. It is at the base of all financial, political, administrative scandals. It is responsible for mercenary marriages, which fill the law courts, pollute society, and contaminate the home.

The poverty of the masses paralyses the efforts of honest industries, honest trades, and honest professions. The men who succeed are not those who benefit their fellow-men, but those who ruthlessly trample them under foot in their heedless race for gold. It is a well-known fact that the upper classes are not prolific, and would die out were they not recruited from the ranks; if therefore the state of the masses is such as to allow its worst element to rise to influential positions in society, demoralization of the masses must inevitably produce demoralization of the classes.

We will leave it to the thinking public to consider to what extent other conditions of the masses, besides poverty, react in all countries on the upper classes—what the effects are, first on the masses, and then on the classes, of corrupt and retrograde churches, compulsory service in the army, police tyranny, bad and unjust laws, tutelage under pragmatical Philistines, caste institutions, official newspapers, State-regulated arts and entertainments, administrative favouritism, etc.

But Max Nordau takes no heed of such all-powerful causes of corruption. He sees degeneration only in the upper classes, and, placing the cart before the horse, he regards what he considers the degenerated author and artist as the cause of a state of affairs of which they are the very last products.

There are many passages in his book that strongly suggest that he is not completely sincere in his one-sided view. The savage blows he sometimes deals at the Anarchists bear witness that this form of—as he would call it—degeneration among the masses caused him a considerable amount of uneasiness. Judging by the similarity of his language and that of the Emperor of Germany, he might well be commissioned to brand both Socialists and Anarchists as wild beasts. Be this as it may, his few allusions to the corruption of the masses serve to enhance the untrustworthiness of the signs of degeneration which he points out in the upper classes.

Among these figure prominently—who would believe it?—modern female toilets. And why? Not because they are indecent, as they have often been in other periods, but because they are eccentric. Is there then a normal dress for ladies? Or what code is there in existence to which Max Nordau can appeal? Is it a sign of degeneration to hold that one of the chief objects of toilets is to be beautiful and to enhance the beauty of the wearer? And ought a lady who dresses according to this principle to be put down as a dweller on the border-land of madness? If women love to dress well, and men love to behold them well-dressed, would it not be madness to adopt ugly and monotonous toilets?

It is, of course, not difficult to see that the author's standard of female toilet is the plain and ugly dress of the German housewife, and that he has never realized the delight which an Englishman takes in seeing his wife richly dressed, and in a way that suits her face and form. If Max Nordau's standard of female dress is the severe draperies of the antique, he does not say so. But, if it be, we must remind him that the beauty of the classic draperies was borrowed from the beauty of the forms they revealed or partly displayed.

With the best will, we could not in northern Europe emulate the Greeks in dress. There are two objections: the climate, which demands warm covering; the sense of may-be false modesty, inherited from the early Christian ages, which prevents the display of human forms. The time will no doubt come when humanity is sufficiently pure-minded—sufficiently degenerated, as Max Nordau would probably say—to dress in clinging draperies, to expose the form more freely indoors and in warm weather; and who would say that morality would not be the gainer? A movement in this direction is already apparent. The skirt-dance represents one stage. The appearance of an actress without shoes or stockings might well herald a return to sandals, and the abandonment of the barbarous fashion of cramping children's feet in pointed shoes.

But to call the women of European society degenerate because, under the present circumstances, they do not go about in light tunics, displaying their feet, their arms, and one leg, is hardly fair.

Our great alienist is very severe on the men of society as well, more especially for the manner in which they trim their beards. We cannot help sympathizing with men who wear a double-pointed beard when they are told that they are on the high road to lunacy because they ape Lucius Verrius, a gentleman whose portrait they have probably never seen. Such stigmata of folly could have been pointed out only by a man whose mind is completely devoid of a sense of the ridiculous.

To anybody who has not a special point to prove at all cost, it will be patent that throughout the whole course of history educated men never dressed more soberly than now. In this matter English fashion governs the world, and the ruling ideas in Englishmen's dress are durability, comfort, and adaptability to the occasions on which it is worn. Continental men may not adhere so strictly to these ideas, but there is good reason to believe that in a short time they will do so.

Modern room and house decorations are, according to Max Nordau, so many indications of degeneration and decay. That there are many rooms and houses eccentrically furnished and decorated throughout the civilized world no one would deny. But compared with the number of houses and rooms chastely furnished and decorated in a manner which is incomparably more pleasant and attractive than the average rooms, especially in Germany and England thirty years ago, these abodes of eccentrics sink into insignificance. As to the decoration of public halls and places of amusement, we surely notice an improvement which could not point to degeneration. Hardly in any European town would such wall decorations be now permitted as disfigured the walls of public places of amusement and dancing-halls in Germany some thirty years ago—the Apollo Saal of Hamburg, to wit, the walls of which represented hell in the worst taste possible.

Here, again, Max Nordau gives us no standard to go by. He does not tell us what the house or the room of a rational being should be like, or to what extent a wealthy man may indulge in a freak, or amuse his friends by grotesque furniture and bizarre decorations, without being degenerated.

The enjoyments of society especially present symptoms which cause our psychologist to tremble for the sanity of the upper classes. Under this head, we expected him to say something of the increasing taste for healthy games and sport, for travel, and the amateur practice of the arts for amusement's sake. Had he been willing to look at the question from both sides, he might have said something about the increasing love of science, especially social science; of good books as well as bad ones; of the high prices fetched by the paintings of the old masters, even those not belonging to the pre-Raphaelite period, consequently real works of art according to Max Nordau. He might have acknowledged the improved tone in social gatherings and the marked diminution in convivial drunkenness.

While sitting in judgment upon the upper classes of Europe, why should he not have noticed the more serious side of their lives as well as their enjoyments, as manifested in subscriptions to hospitals or orphanages, and institutes of every description; sick-nursing establishments, where ladies of high rank and wealth give their personal services, sacrifices of time and comfort in the endeavour to brighten the lives of the poor, to save fallen women, to assist released prisoners, to protect children and even animals from cruelty? We say, purposely, nothing of all the charitable work done in connection with churches, because Max Nordau and his admirers might not recognise any results of religious feeling as a proof of sanity.

But all these emphatic and unmistakable indications of the state of society—at least as valuable as the manifestations of vice, hysteria, and eccentricity —are ignored. On the other hand, he makes much of the attempts which here and there have been made, especially in Paris, with representations appealing to many senses at once ; for instance, pictures exhibited with music, musical recitals in darkened rooms, etc. Such cases are not only extremely rare, but simply are another combination of many arts hardly more complicated than that represented by operas, in which dance music, poetry, and painting are mingled in order to please.

In what recorded period, and in what nation, have there not been attempts to create new sources of enjoyment? Why should not attempts be made at advance in amusements as well as in any other feature of our civilization ? That many of these experiments appear silly, and end in utter failure, ought to surprise nobody, and scientists the least. Any one who has tried to invent something new, to ascertain by experiments some scientific fact, or to solve a physical or mechanical problem, ought to know that a very large number of experiments are bound to fail before success is achieved. It is strange to find in our days a scientist condemning, as the beginning of folly, that dissatisfaction with existing things which is the primary motor of all progress and all knowledge. By doing so he ranges himself on the side of those Philistines who burnt the apostles of progress as heretics and imprisoned the pioneers of science as madmen.

The unrest which our psychologist notices in the educated classes exists as well among all the lower classes of Europe, though among them it reveals itself in other manifestations. It springs however from the same source—a strong instinctive feeling, largely corroborated by judgment, that human life in all spheres is, in the present epoch, utterly out of harmony with nature, with our irresistible instincts, and all those noble aspirations, on the realization of which our self-respect, our ease of mind, and our happiness alone can be based. It is not alone the present feeling of incongruity which disturbs humanity, but the fast-ripening conviction that we are moving in a wrong direction inspires despair, pessimism in some, and a desire for hazardous new departures in others.

This sense of unrest, this craving for change, far from being symptoms of degeneration, are the first faint indications of renewing vitality. If decay there be, it is simply the fermentation which precedes germination.

Two opposing principles, two different systems, two classes of antagonistic institutions, cannot exist in the same place and at the same time. When therefore old things have been tried *ad nauseam* and constantly found wanting, any unprejudiced man, nay, even an animal, must experience a desire to destroy them. This feeling naturally becomes strongest in the man with an imaginative and aspiring mind : for besides the general disgust of old things, he sees in them the chief obstacles to better and higher things. The axe must precede the plough, because the forest cannot co-exist with the wheat-field. The growing enmity against old dogmas, old authorities, old forms among the educated and artistic classes, the kindling rage of the masses against existing institutions, signal the clearing of the rank jungle and the pestilential swamps prior to cultivation. The leading features of modern culture have up till now been submission to authorities, violation of nature, sacrifice of individual liberty, and progression on Collectivist lines. What wonder then that those who keenly feel the present degradation of man, achieved under old conditions, should turn against these and clamour for liberty, nature, and self?

Max Nordau, with his German-Philistine ideas, with his head crammed full of authoritative teaching, and biassed by the clap-trap of the commonest Collectivism, has utterly misunderstood the phenomena which he has only partially observed. He does not allow for the mistakes, the exaggerations, and the eccentricities committed by men who try to give expression to their feelings, their yearnings, their aspirations, unhampered by traditional bonds. He is bewildered because a movement springing entirely from feeling and instinct does not follow a fixed programme, or some dry philosophical system. He under-estimates the value of an ethical revolution, because so far it has not reached its constructive stage ; and because the new apostles of liberty, intoxicated by their self-liberation, run amuck indiscriminately against all old things, be they good or bad ; because the movement is in the hands of extremists, enthusiasts, and sentimentalists, and still awaits the guiding hand of the unbiassed logician, the cool-headed sociologist and economist, capable of harmonizing it with practical life and moral order.

Max Nordau, by his book, has forfeited his claim to be one of these.

CHAPTER III

MYSTICISM AND THE UNKNOWABLE

OF the good things contained in Max Nordau's book which should secure for it a place in the study of every educated man, his fourth chapter entitled " Etiology" figures conspicuously. He deals here with the causes—not the primary economic and sociological causes, but the immediate causes—of the increasing bodily debilities and mental derangements characteristic of our epoch. Such facts, or generally assumed facts, as that the average term of human life is extending; that the average stature of man has increased since the middle ages, rendering the armour of mighty men of those days too small for middle-sized men of our generation; that the average chest-measure in the German army is expanding; that personal beauty of children, women, and men is in the ascendant; that many men attain to a great age without the slightest sign of diminished mental power;—all these facts might appear so many contradictions to Max Nordau's assertions in the chapter alluded to.

But, though the consideration of them might induce

him to modify some of the minor points, they are not completely inconsistent with his general reasoning. He warns us that the excessive consumption of spirits and tobacco, the use of opiates and poisons in general, produce debility and premature death. Bad food, bad air, bad dwellings, and a great number of other disadvantages which town dwellers, especially the poor, must endure, are no doubt at least as harmful to body and mind as he proves. He rightly attributes a great number of nerve diseases to the prostration and fatigue consequent upon over-exertion and over excitement, which seems inevitable in an epoch of railways, telegraphs, and machinery.

The whole of his chapter "Etiology," however, dealing as it does with the degeneration of the masses, seems to contradict what he says in his first chapter about the upper classes only being affected by *fin de siècle* degeneration, while the masses experience only a more or less slight touch of it. It also seems to disprove his theory that degenerate authors and artists are the chief cause of degeneration among the upper classes, a view which leads him to overlook the most palpable and most powerful causes for the production of those psychological phenomena throughout civilized humanity which he notices only among the upper classes.

In discussing degeneration it is of the utmost importance to know how the affliction progresses—

whether certain authors and artists were degenerated, and then affected the upper classes — or whether the upper classes were degenerated and thus produced the degenerated authors and artists. Max Nordau seems to vacillate between the two opinions, or he considers the pernicious influence to have been reciprocal. It is however clear that he regards these authors and artists, as well as those members of the upper classes who sympathize with them, as dwellers on the borderland between sanity and madness. The stigmata, or the signs of distorted minds, he divides—as they necessarily must be divided—into bodily stigmata and mental stigmata. The bodily stigmata are of course malformations of the head, and he lays particular stress on the conformation of the ear, its more or less projecting position, the shape of the lobe, or its clinging to the head. It would have been charity and justice on his part to have explained that, while these stigmata are frequently found on lunatics and idiots, there are probably millions of people who bear them without being demented, or even eccentric.

On the other hand, it cannot be denied that there are thousands of lunatics who possess well-shaped heads and ears.

He relies however but little on the bodily stigmata, and finds them only on a few of his subjects. He deals, of course, chiefly with the mental stigmata, and among these he gives mysticism a prominent place. He quotes from Legrain to the effect that "mystical thoughts are to be laid to the account of insanity and degeneration," but Legrain adds at once that they are observable in two states—in epilepsy and in hysterical delirium. According to his authority we consequently know that those who suffer from epilepsy and delirium are apt to be mystical. But Legrain would probably be the first to object to the conclusion that all those who are mystically inclined suffer from epilepsy and delirium.

In his definition of mysticism Max Nordau says that "the word describes a state of mind in which the subject imagines that he sees or divines unknown and inexplicable relations amongst phenomena, discerns in things hints at mysteries, and regards them as symbols." But he adds, "by which dark powers seek to unveil, or, at least, to indicate all sorts of marvels which he endeavours to guess, though generally in vain."

We have divided his definition into two parts, because placed in one sentence it seems an incorrect and unfair definition, the former part of which might be used as a proof of degeneration in a perfectly sound mind, while the latter part is the essential of the whole definition.

As we have already pointed out, science and all researches have utterly failed to furnish replies to all questions regarding the origin, aim, plan, and final destiny of the universe and of humanity. Under such circumstances, the world around us, that which has preceded it, that which will follow it, as well as ourselves, necessarily remain mysteries. Can then any one who perceives or divines unknown, and to us now inexplicable, relations between phenomena and who discerns mysteries be regarded as a degenerate? All the scientific facts of which we are now in possession were mysteries before they were discovered, and the scientists who, guided by slight hints and sometimes by guesses, have unravelled the marvels of nature, could not surely be put down as lunatics. It is therefore evident that the phrase "dark power" is a most essential part in Max Nordau's definition, and that a man can behold mysteries, dwell on them, study them, sometimes unravel them, and remain a perfectly sane man, and that he only who is mystical and deals with mysteries in an irrational way is a degenerate.

Max Nordau says as much in his illustration of the peasant who is a mystic in his religion and in his belief in the weather-witch, but a matter-of-fact man in his farming and his business. But he is not so lenient to the exponents of the mystic school in art and literature. With regard to these, he is rather prone to determine the state of their mind according to that part of a quotation from Morel which he has italicised in his book, "*a morbid deviation from an original type.*" The word morbid alone would have sufficed, but he seems to attach more importance to the other part of the sentence and to regard all who deviate from an original type as degenerate. He does not allow for extenuating circumstances in the authors and artists as he does in the case of the peasant. If he did, he could not class any of these, or their admirers, among the degenerates, unless he could also prove that they were irrational in their daily life and their business relations.

He acknowledges that the emotional nature of man has played a more important part in the world than his intellect, and yet he seems to have before his eyes an original type consisting exclusively of intellect and devoid of emotions. If man's destiny, his moral condition, his education, his happiness, and his usefulness in the world, were to be determined chiefly by his intellectual power, the progress of the race would have been infinitely more slow than it has been, and the bulk of individuals now alive would be far less removed from the animal than they are.

It might be contended that, if not all, at least a large number of religions have brought with them many evils, but, taking a broad view of the work accomplished by them in comparison, not with what they would have done had they been more perfect, but with that state which would have prevailed had they never existed, no unprejudiced historian will deny that civilization and the progress of our race have been considerably accelerated through the influence of religions.

No religion is based on logic, and hardly ever were religious precepts and dogmas accepted exclusively on intellectual grounds. Faith and reasoning, considerably modified by emotion, have always formed the basis of religious beliefs.

Not only in connection with religious matters, but in every event and every development in human affairs, emotion has played an active and prominent part. Such feelings as love, friendship, ambition, lust, gratitude, hatred, revengefulness, patriotism, loyalty, chivalry, etc., are the great motive powers in the human drama, and when the intellect steps in it is as their counsellor and their servant.

It is therefore legitimate and reasonable for those who wish to sway human beings, who wish to educate them, elevate them, to address themselves to their emotional nature. In the position in which man is placed—living on a cosmic grain of sand, moving in space by an inexplicable power at an inconceivable speed, without knowing who he is and why he is—the mystical must perforce have a great attraction for him. To be easily impressed by the mystical is therefore one of his natural conditions, be it good, bad, or indifferent. When the emotional nature of human beings is appealed to it is as rational for artists and poets to address themselves to the love of the mystical as to the love of the beautiful, and therefore there should be a legitimate place for mysticism in art and poetry.

It is almost inconceivable that an educated, well-balanced mind should never dwell on those immensities still unexplored, and the innumerable enigma still unsolved or insoluble, and content itself with lingering over those comparatively insignificant truths which science so far has revealed. To what an extent a man remains satisfied with quasi-explanations of scientific research depends on the strength of his imagination. It is pardonable if alienists should look upon imagination as a doubtful blessing; but though it may appear a dangerous gift in their patients, there can be little doubt that it is an indispensable attribute to a well-equipped mind. It is the mental faculty which most distinguishes man from the animals—the one on which he could with the greatest appearance of legitimacy base his claim to divine origin. Dogs may dream and horses may see ghosts, but their hallucinations are vastly different from the imagination of man, which allows him to receive and retain almost any number of presentations, to elaborate them into new combinations, thus reconstructing pictures of the past and daring conceptions of the future, capable of easy realization. A powerful imagination is essential not only to the poet and the artist, but to the engineer, the mechanician, the statesman,—in fact, to all who set themselves a practical task or a distinct ideal.

It is the imaginative strength of the scientist which renders him a pioneer and a discoverer, and without it he is to his science what the performer of music who cannot compose is to music. From everyday experience we are justified in believing that the cramming of the memory, that much reading for examinations, or other purposes, and a developed habit of relying on authorities, tends to weaken the imagination in a man. This seems to be confirmed by the theory of psychologists: that desuetude of a faculty tends to its decay; and might well be the explanation of the often-confirmed fact that great discoverers and inventors have seldom emerged from the ranks of the omnivorous readers of the universities.

In the same manner we may explain what we have before called the scientific superstition discernible in so many scientists. The more they are satisfied with their systems, the more they take nomenclature and classification for adequate explanation, the less they are attracted by the spheres into which science has not penetrated or cannot penetrate. There is this similarity between the scientifically superstitious and the theologically superstitious—that they both believe that they have explained all, and they thereby place themselves beyond the possibility of being right; for the mass of unexpected facts revealed by science, eclipsing as they do the wildest flight of the imagination, renders it possible for any man to be right in his speculations on the secrets of the universe save those men who say that they know all.

It is therefore not surprising that a scientist by erudition, and especially an alienist, who, by dint of studying the mechanism which connects what some call the soul, and others designate as the trinity of the consciousness, the judgment and will, with the body, has persuaded himself that there is nothing beyond nerves, cells and the grey matter, should look with contempt on imagination, and yet more so on the love of the mystical, and that his ideal man, his "original type," should possess so little imagination as to remain unaffected by the mystical.

Lack of information and of observation has caused the multitude to regard a great number of men—distinguished in the eyes of the world exclusively by their intellectual powers—as non-mystics to such a degree as to class them as atheists. The majority of such men, though distinctly at variance with the dogmas and views of established sects, have been and are in their inner consciousness, both mystics and religionists. When in public they have seemingly attacked religion and mysticism, they have in reality only attacked churches and superstition. In the judgment of a great many intelligent men the controversy between Professor Huxley and Dr. Martineau goes far to confirm this view. When humanity, including scientists, learns to distinguish between religion and churches, it will be understood that almost all men in the past and present, who have deservedly been called great, have been religionists, and therefore mystics.

Let us instance Faraday. He belonged all his life to a sect which must be classed among the mystics, and he died a believer in its creed. Are we then to class this keen observer, accurate investigator and brilliant logician, this daring pioneer of science, this ingenious unraveller of Nature's secrets, among the degenerates? If we do, where should we class average scientists, including Max Nordau? Or should we place ourselves in the position of the common-sense German Philistine, and declare that mysticism is not mysticism when it takes the shape of the belief of a sect tolerated by the police?

But is not Faraday's mysticism perfectly compatible with a sound mind? He was one of those scientists with unclouded reasoning powers, whose knowledge — gained by investigation, not from authorities—had taught him how little he knew of the great mysteries of creation. He recognised that our emotional cravings cannot be satisfied by science in its present stage, but only by emotional realization. Hence his religious attitude towards the great mysterious power of which he knew nothing, but whose work became more and more manifest as his investigation proceeded. What wiser course could a man adopt, who was so capable of distinguishing essence from form, than to give that form to his religion which had gratified his emotional nature as a child?

If sound minds may be mystically inclined, if our emotional nature can be reached by mysticism in poetry and art, and if our emotions are acknowledged to be receptive to elevating and pleasing impressions, the pre-Raphaelites could not all have been as degenerate as Max Nordau would have us believe. They were, no doubt, emotionalists, mystics and even symbolists, and they frankly claimed the right to be regarded as such. They considered themselves as having a mission, and the fact that a man throws himself heart and soul into his mission is no sign of degeneration.

Now, there are walks in life, callings, missions, which involve no risk to those who undertake them; there are others that involve great risks.

Some callings expose a man to bodily harm, others to mental harm. Nothing could be more uncharitable and cruel than to revile a man, to attack his reputation, to wound his feelings and to lower his self-esteem, because he returns maimed and invalided after having fought the good fight.

A shopkeeper, a shoemaker, an author of sensational books, runs but little risk of damaging either his body or his mind. The sailor, the miner, the leader of a revolution, exposes himself to great bodily danger. The man who acquires a vast erudition may dull his imagination and his judgment; the man who strains his brain to the utmost, who, perhaps, overstrains it, in the solution of difficult problems, the man whose mission lies in the domain of the emotions exposes his mind to injury. If there be truth in this, mysticism in poetry and art may cause degeneration in the poet's or the artist's mind, especially if it be a weak one; but to conclude from this that mysticism in art springs from diseased minds is to confound cause with effect.

If we accept Max Nordau's Philistine definition of art and his views as to its mission, mysticism would have no place in art or in poetry. He would certainly exclude it, but in doing so he would contradict himself glaringly. We have already complained that he does not explain his standards, and that he does not give us his ideals. But from his work before us, it is evident that the standard by which he would measure poetry is the work of Goethe and Shakespeare, especially the former. Goethe owes his fame largely to his "Faust,"—a mystical work if ever there was one. The prologue is religious mysticism, the first part is diabolism, the second part is archmysticism, which so far has resisted all attempts at interpretation. In the same manner "Hamlet," "Macbeth," and other plays of Shakespeare derive their great charm and their artistic value largely from mysticism.

All this however does not prove that either irrational or dishonest mysticism is acceptable, and much that Max Nordau says regarding pre-Raphaelitism should be taken to heart by the camp-followers of the movement. In this term we include, of course, those painters who, unable to draw and paint, try to force their pictures upon the market by sheer bounce; and empty-headed critics who insolently assume a mental, or, as they would call it, a spiritual, superiority by writing obscure, unintelligible rigmaroles in praise of pictures which attract attention by means of nought but their eccentricity. This class of people cannot be considered as representing the pre-Raphaelite movement, nor can they be called degenerate in the sense Max Nordau means, for there is a method in their degeneracy which yields pounds, shillings and pence. We also include in this category a class of people whose conceit may border on degeneracy, and who believe that any one who cannot draw and paint is qualified for a pre-Raphaelite painter, and who sincerely assume and enjoy the position as misunderstood geniuses.

As to the crowds in the exhibitions that gather before an incomprehensible eccentricity made conspicuous by the log-rolling process, they surely do not all deserve the epithet of degenerates. Many are drawn there by sheer curiosity; others damn with faint praise, in order to escape the wrath of the fanatic. There are also, of course, many who, for the purpose of giving themselves airs, admire traits of beauty which they really fail to see. The behaviour of these hypocritical æsthetes is, of course, deplorable, but they yield to a weakness not confined to the end of our century. Andersen's story of the king's clothes, inspired by a very old German tale, is one of many evidences of the antiquity of such folly.

The sincere pre-Raphaelites deserve the sympathy of every thinking man, though they may be guilty of many imperfections. According to Max Nordau, the mission of the painter is to serve as a vehicle of beautiful impressions to the public. A man who fulfilled this mission might indeed be called an artist, and his painting might be the limits of painting as such. But this does not prevent a picture from containing a story, a moral, or the expression of an emotion, if the painter be a good story-teller, a true poet, and a sound teacher. If a work of art can thus fulfil two high purposes instead of one, everybody is a gainer by it, and the fact that it is the embodiment of two arts instead of one cannot reasonably be made an objection. The artist who succeeds in thus blending two arts should surely not be called a degenerate.

Ruskin did not, as Max Nordau confesses, advocate any neglect in the art of painting as such, but he warned artists not to waste their time on unworthy subjects. He is a philanthropist as well as a writer on art, and feels aggrieved when the artist neglects so good an opportunity of teaching as a well-executed painting offers, and yet more when he sees art abased in order to gratify sensuality or morbid cravings for the horrible.

That Ruskin did not so absolutely disregard beautiful pictures which have no story to tell and no teaching to impart becomes incontestible when we remember his panegyrics of Turner.

Victor Hugo in his "Notre Dame de Paris" makes Claude Frollo say, when he has a book in his hand and the old cathedral before him, that the one will kill the other, meaning, of course, that books were predestined to supersede symbolism in buildings and other arts. Max Nordau takes for granted that this has already been done. He sees no good in works of art giving expression to ideas and emotions which could so much better be described and more clearly defined in books. But is there not a great inconsistency in first admitting that art keeps within its rational limit when it presents the beauties of nature to the public in such a manner as to make them more evident, which is equal to teaching that nature is beautiful, and then to say that art oversteps its limits when it teaches, or attempts to teach, anything else?

If we survey all the means available to humanity for the conveyance of thoughts and emotions, they present a scale which begins by speech and ends with music. Though it must be acknowledged that speech only with difficulty lends itself to the expression of one or a considerable number of interdependent and intertangent complex ideas perfectly clear in a sound mind, it is however the best means we possess for lucid expression. Written prose has the same merit as speech, and may be used to express the driest mathematical facts, as well as the most poetical imaginings. Verse, we think it will be generally allowed, is better calculated to convey poetical ideas and expressions, as it admits of greater liberty, more stirring language, bolder metaphors, and because rhythm and rhyme, in virtue of their musical qualities, appeal to the imagination and stir the emotions.

When to poetry melody is added, it becomes song, a mode of expression which appeals fully as much to our emotional nature as to our intellect. When instrumental music is added to song, to evoke emotion becomes the cardinal object, and intellect receives hardly any impression. Music without words is the mode of conveying emotions—and possibly ideas, too subtle, so to say, too spiritual to be analysed by the intellect—in so distinct a way that the emotions of the composer, and may be of the performer, are faithfully reproduced in the hearers. A mutual understanding is thus established between them as clearly as any understanding arrived at through exhaustive verbal explanation.

Scientists have endeavoured to explain on materialist lines the charm exercised by music over us, but their explanations obviously never touch more than the mechanical motion of the sound-waves and the receptive mechanism of the ear and the brain. Their dogmatizing is moreover so dry, halting, and one-sided as to convince musical people that their attempt at explanation is hopeless. Music belongs to the sphere of emotions, which lie beyond the ken of science, and will be as long as scientific progression is hampered by the materialist bias.

And yet the most unimaginative scientist will not

deny that all the methods of conveying ideas and emotions enumerated in the above scale, including instrumental music, are legitimate arts. Why then should there not be the same latitude allowed to the arts appealing to us through the sight as to those appealing to us through the hearing? If the architect, sculptor, or painter, or two of them, or even three of them, combined in collaboration, wishing to convey an impression, or to evoke an emotion, why should they not be allowed to do so by any of the means which fall within their sphere? If they should wish to evoke emotions similar to those evoked by music, and they can do so by choosing a certain subject, by introducing certain symbols, or even by recalling sentiments of the past—the time of our first love, our youth, or even our childhood—why should they not be free to do so?

The pre-Raphaelites claim the freedom to thus expand the scope of pictorial art, to sanctify it, and to make it appeal to the inmost recesses of our emotional nature; and as the movement was started at a time when art was in decadence and tended to become subservient, abroad to pruriency, and at home, to abominable Philistinism, the pre-Raphaelites deserve a better treatment than they have received at the hands of Max Nordau.

That they should commit mistakes was inevitable. It is probable that they had not realized completely to themselves the exact results to be aimed at. Like the composer of music, they wished to convey to others such of their own emotions as they deemed legitimate, beautiful, and ennobling, and had to grope in the dark, or to trust to momentary inspiration, for the means. Being, and wishing to be emotional, they may have neglected their intellectual powers, forgetting that even when emotion reigns supreme it can express itself truly only by the aid of intelligence. Vivid emotions and powerful imaginations are not in themselves stigmata of degeneration, but rather the signs of a rich mind, so long as they remain under the control of the intellect. It is only when they run riot, unheeding the criticism of intellect, that the balance of the mind is imperilled.

In their desire to emphasize the spiritual meaning and the emotional nature of their works, the pre-Raphaelites may have committed the mistake of neglecting execution, truthfulness to nature, and the laws of optics. Finding pictures appreciated by the public in virtue of the subject and the conception, despite faulty treatment, many of them no doubt have been induced to realize their ideas and emotions on canvas before they had sufficiently trained their eye and their hand.

Every educated Englishman will understand that Max Nordau somewhat distorts facts and conveys wrong impressions in the account he gives of the movement. Though the pre-Raphaelite Brotherhood was dissolved, the movement has not been so devoid of results as he insinuates. Though the first exhibition of the Brotherhood was also the last one, pictures by the same artists have been constantly exhibited, and some of them have fetched fabulous prices. He says that Millais, amongst others, has retained that characteristic of the pre-Raphaelite Brotherhood consisting of minuteness in details, draperies, and backgrounds. Any one who has seen Millais' striking portraits, his "Cherry Ripe," "Bubbles," "Coller Herrings," and other pictures could not possibly make such an assertion. We must, of course, allow for the circumstance that Max Nordau's knowledge of the pictures he criticises is second-hand.

It is evident that he has not seen Millais' latest pictures. Had he done so, he would not have jeopardized his whole system of reasoning by holding Millais up as an example of degeneration. Here, as in many other cases, Max Nordau, while exhibiting an enormous erudition, reveals a remarkable want of logic. To call Millais degenerate is a desperate way out of a dilemma in which he has landed himself by asserting, on the one hand, that those who paint pictures such as Millais painted years ago are people with degenerate brains, and, on the other, that people who produce pictures such as Millais paints now are people of sound mind. If degeneration is the first step towards a high, normal and sound development, Max Nordau has been guilty of much ado about nothing.

Had he ever beheld Holman Hunt's "Shadow of the Cross" even in an engraving, he could not in his description of it have committed the mistakes he has unless his mind is impervious to pictorial impressions. He says that "the shadow of his (Christ's) body falling on the ground shows the form of a cross." This is not true. The shadow of Christ's body falls on the wall, where a tool shelf and suspended tools simulate a cross. Max Nordau's erroneous description will certainly prejudice those, who have not seen the picture, against Holman Hunt.

It is natural that the materialist, the pseudo-scientifically superstitious, and the Philistine tendencies of our age, so eminently embodied in the mind of Max Nordau, and against which the pre-Raphaelite school is a protest, should militate against a fair appreciation of the tentative departure of these innovators.

The essence of their mysticism and their symbolism is in their belief in what, for lack of a better term, has been called their spiritual life—the belief that the mind is not a condition of matter, but that our thinking *Ego* might have existed before it was incarnated, and that it will live after our body has decayed. Could our earthly existence be proved finite with certainty, could any future existence be proved a vain dream, incompatible with reason, then indeed would pre-Raphaelitism be the beginning of folly, as, in fact, would most of the things which now tend to lighten and beautify our lives. We shall not here endeavour to determine the five-thousand-year-old discussion regarding eternal life. We shall simply point out that the proofs on which the so-called materialists base their conclusions are not so absolutely convincing as to stigmatize their opponents as lunatics.

Any one who has glanced at the development of science from old times up to the present is well aware of that weakness in the mind of scientists—especially the non-pioneer scientists—which induces them to believe that the conclusions they have arrived at, generally in opposition to predecessors, are the whole truth and nothing but the truth. For thousands of years it has been the same. For each step that science has climbed upwards, its votaries, with a few brilliant exceptions, have believed themselves to be at the top, and have with scorn rejected, as sheer folly, any suggestion that the step on which they stand is rotten and that there are sounder steps higher up. The scientists of other days in their turn looked upon Columbus, Galileo, and Tycho Brahe as fools. A hundred years ago the scientists would have laughed to scorn any one who had told them that their senses deceived them with regard to light, darkness, colours, silence and sound, and that all these presentations received by our senses were simply movement or manifestations of energy. The theory which regarded atoms as minute subdivisions of matter is quite a modern dogma, and yet it is already tottering to its fall. More rational scientists already speak of atoms as centres of force, an expression which twenty years ago was regarded as rank heresy. If the theory that atoms are centres of force is accepted, with all its consequences, science is on the threshold of a new departure which may cause the materialists to look small indeed; for if what to our senses appears as matter is a condition of force, instead of force being a condition of matter, a vista entirely opposite to that of the materialists is open to science—a vista disclosing possibilities before which we might well stand in awe.

Though it is incontestable that invention and discovery have been enormously accelerated by often apparently wild suggestions by the imagination, by emotion, and by instinct, it is especially such suggestions which are visited by the most furious onslaughts on the part of the superstitious scientists. When these reject as utter folly imaginings prompted by faith or any other emotions, it is because such suggestions are not only entirely out of harmony with the scientific ideas of the moment, but because they appear so extraordinary, so utterly destructive to the views familiar to them. They would be less positive in face of suggestions and speculations justified by emotion, if they did not constantly forget that every scientific discovery reveals facts which are not only diametrically opposed to opinions previously held, but also so marvellous as to baffle human understanding. Bearing recent scientific discovery in mind, no one will deny the folly of the man who a hundred years ago would have prophetically declared, "What we now have proved true and reasonable will in a hundred years be proved error and folly, and what to us now appears as sheer madness and rank impossibility will then be scientific truth."

Any contemporary scientist, unaffected by scientific superstition, would unhesitatingly acknowledge the probability of present scientific dogmas being declared errors, and that what would now appear as the hallucinations of an overheated imagination may become scientific truth a century hence.

Though the narrow-minded scientist who takes up his stand on the so far explored speck of the universe has no right to blame the artist or poet who, guided by emotion and faith, plunges his imagination into the surrounding abyss of the mystical, which no well-balanced mind can ignore, it would be both unjust and absurd to blame the prosaic and plodding scientist who concentrates his whole mind on scientific details, and, to use a happy metaphor of Max Nordau himself, is building a bridge, arch by arch, out into the unknown. It is good that the Alpine climber should concentrate his attention on the steps he hews in the ice and the safe resting-point he can find for his feet, and not allow his mind to wander in the dark precipice below him or among the lofty peaks he hopes to reach. Man being two personalities, one emotional, the other intellectual, stands in need of the services of both the logical scientist and the emotional artist and poet.

Once it has been recognised that the emotions may be conveyed by pictorial art, we cannot quarrel with the *raison d'être* of the pre-Raphaelites, though we might disagree with them as to the means they are using. They can however justly demand that those who criticise their means of expression should show the possibility of better ones. Holman Hunt has aimed at evoking by his pictures a feeling of respect and admiration for religion, and in many cases has succeeded; and the means he has employed are a reverential treatment, a style of old associated with religious representations and suggestions of the supernatural. Burne Jones, whose object seems to be to emphasize the higher significance of our spiritual being over our bodily, does so by giving us pictures of maidens whose beauty is of a kind devoid of all those attractions which coquetry, roguishness, animal spirits, and exuberance of health may confer. Their vacant and inward look suggests a contemplative mood and a yearning to see the invisible. As if to still further quicken the sluggish imagination of the masses, he cloaks his figures in draperies and surrounds them by objects which of old have been used in representing holy people. He comes as near as possible to the representation of wingless angels, without presenting anything that could not be seen in reality.

Such pictures may not appeal to everybody, but we have overwhelming evidence that they do appeal to a great number ; and if the belief in a superiority over animals, in a spiritual personality, in a responsibility for our development, and in a future life, contributes to our happiness and exercises an ennobling influence on our race, the pictures of Burne Jones cannot be the work of a degenerate aiming at the degeneration of others.

What by many is considered Rossetti's masterpiece, " Dante's Dream," would by a painter, in his capacity of craftsman, be found to contain many defects, and only one great merit—exquisite colouring. The conception is eccentric, the surroundings are symbolic and mystical, and the anatomy is incorrect. There are faults of perspective, some of them glaring. For instance, the left shoulder of the angel of love who stands on the left hand of Beatrice, facing her and bending over her, is partly hidden by Beatrice's right shoulder, which could not be possible in reality unless the two figures had only two dimensions—height and breadth, with no thickness. And yet this picture has been bought by the Corporation of Liverpool for a large sum, and is considered as a thing of joy and beauty by a mass of people among whom Max Nordau could detect but a few with malformations of the heads and the ears, and who in the whole of their life have given abundant proof of practical rationalism far greater even than that of the superstitious peasant he instances as having a sound mind.

The charm of the picture does not lie in the execution, but in the conception. It is probable that it evokes exactly the same emotion felt by Rossetti while painting it. The subject being a dream, the many symbols tend to throw the spectator into the mood in which the picture should be contemplated. There is an atmosphere of Sabbath—presentiment of bliss—which is produced by the introduction of such presentations which in our youth or childhood have been associated with that day. The artist has succeeded in intensifying the belief in the sacredness of love and the consolations which, amid the troubles of life, may be drawn from the faith in a spiritual existence.

The conceiving and representing of pictures like this, the outcome of intense emotion, might well endanger the balance of the painter's mind, but the soothing influence they exercise on the spectator would surely assuage rather than excite any restless mind which, deprived of a profound philosophy and a far-reaching scientific knowledge, must needs cling to faith.

The painter who produces on the canvas a beautiful scene from nature, beautiful flowers, or other beautiful objects, pleases and elevates the beholders of the picture. Max Nordau admits as much. But he does not analyse the methods by which this result is accomplished. He would probably not deny that one of the feelings which such a picture calls forth is a sympathy with nature and the Creator, and that this sympathy favours the conception of the distinct idea that the great power of the universe suggested by natural beauties—as the painter is suggested by the picture—loves the beautiful, and consequently the good.

The signification of the pre-Raphaelites in the progress of art is that they strive to teach, in the production of groups and figures, similar emotions and thoughts to those produced by the representation of natural beauties. They have therefore contributed considerably to the elevation of art so far as aims and subjects go. If they believe that a purpose can be attained only by the imitation of the unskilled pre-Raphaelite painters, by violating nature, by eliminating perspective and by apotheosizing ugliness, they do not further that regeneration which we believe they are striving for. But there is every reason to hope that modern art will come out ennobled from the crisis into which it has been plunged, and that rising painters will see their way to paint reverently and realize their noblest aims and highest ideals, represented in naturally beautiful forms, painted with the greatest skill of a painter proud of his craft.

Whether this hope be realized or not, it seems to us that a regeneration of art would be impossible without the attempts at new departure which Max Nordau has mistaken for degeneration.

CHAPTER IV

THE BANKRUPTCY OF SCIENCE

IN his chapter entitled "Symbolism," Max Nordau seeks confirmation for his theory of degeneration in the tendency, more or less perceptible all the world over, on the part of contemporary artists and poets, to have recourse to symbols in giving expression to ideas and emotions impossible to convey in ordinary language. Every one who has had to do with intricate syntheses of ideas, even of the driest and the most clearly definable kind, is well aware that language often appears inadequate to convey such syntheses from one mind to another. How much more difficult then must it be to convey in exact language a presentation conjured up from the imagination, an artistic conception, a poetical mood, a strong emotion, or a chord of emotions, to use an expression that may in itself serve as an illustration. The use of symbols, as we have just used the word chord, has not only enormously widened the capability of language, but has rendered it far more lucid, laconic, and agreeable.

A modern orator, or writer, could not possibly

dispense with symbols, for without them his speeches or his books would be intensely wordy, tiresome, and difficult to comprehend. Language is constantly being enriched by new symbols, either invented and introduced by authors, or taken from such literary works as have become classic. Often an author creates a character or an idea which typifies characters and situations frequently met with, and for which symbols have long been needed. Thus, for instance, Andersen's "Ugly Duckling" became a symbol largely used as soon as his fable was published, and when Ibsen's "Doll's House" was played for the first time in London, one newspaper, which, by the way, took Max Nordau's view of Ibsen and declared his characters impossible, in another article, if we remember aright, on the subject of marriage, used with great effect Ibsen's Nora as a symbol.

But such symbols are as old as language, and the new tendency of *littérateurs* who call themselves, or who are called, symbolists, is not to invent and to use symbols that stand for well-known and perfectly undisputed characters and situations, but such as represent new ideas, difficult to define, or undefinable, because incomplete, and concerning emotions. The same authors are also prone to use symbols for things, beings, and powers, the existence of which has not been ascertained by the senses, but simply guessed at, or evolved from consciousness.

Many such symbols were not symbols when first introduced into the language, but nouns that stood for things, or beings, supposed to be perfectly real. Thus, for instance, the word devil, which in olden times stood for a satanic majesty, adorned with horns and tail, has now become a convenient symbol, a thing only too real, but covering such immense ground, and presenting such innumerable aspects, that a symbol expressing the whole conception is extremely convenient. Nothing is commoner than to hear a clergyman use the word "the devil" in his sermon, though it be part of his creed and of his teachings that God is so omnipresent throughout the universe that there is not a square inch for a personal devil to place his foot on.

It is this kind of symbolism which Max Nordau is bent on crucifying as degeneration. As we have already said, there is a general tendency among artists to indulge in it, in order to produce moods and suggest emotions. Thus, for example, in the picture spoken of in our last chapter, "Dante's Dream," an atmosphere of love is represented by red birds, and sleep is represented by poppies strewn on the floor. In Rossetti's picture Max Nordau would have taken objection to such symbols, though he seems reconciled to the symbols used by Raphael and his school, and would probably not object to those of German allegorical painters and sculptors.

It is significant that the symbolism, which he most vehemently holds up as a stigma of degeneration, is that of the modern French poets, who have made religious symbolism their speciality. It is not difficult to see why these have been chosen as the scapegoats for the symbolism of every art and every country. It is true they boldly call themselves symbolists. But this would not be enough to elicit from Max Nordau a chapter of forty-five pages. Besides calling themselves symbolists, they have the audacity to be French. Their symbolism is religious, and, what is worse, is Roman Catholic, and, what is worst of all, it is antagonistic to science.

Though the now prevailing love for symbols does not always manifest itself in a religious way, it is natural for it to find its widest application in speeches and writings on religion. Religion avowedly deals with things not of this earth, is based not on knowledge and investigation, but on faith, and appeals not to our intellect, but to our emotional nature.

The French symbolists have created greater sympathy with their religious views than might have been expected in our rational times because, unlike the Catholic clergy of the past, they treat as symbols what before were considered as representations of actual facts. They are not orthodox; and if the Church of Rome is anxious, as it seems to be, to turn this neo-Catholicism into a means of resuming its influence, it can only do so by enormously modernizing its fundamental ideas. It will be interesting to see whether the Church of Rome will accept the symbolists as co-operators, or finally spurn them as heretics.

What especially rouses the animosity of Max Nordau against the symbolists is the fact that the new movement is based on the supposition that science is bankrupt, or, in other words, that it has failed in all its promises to humanity; that it has usurped the throne of religion under false pretences; and that its incapacity to supplant religion has been demonstrated by the latest scientific discoveries. According to the idea underlying the French symbolist movement, science has during the present century aimed at the destruction of religion, and has caused religion to be neglected, discredited, and scorned.

Such a movement, founded on such premises and aiming at such aims, must be of the greatest interest to any man who watches attentively the development of our race. To study its true cause, its real nature, and its real aims, should be the desire of every earnest investigator; and if Max Nordau falls back on obloquy, indelicate insinuations, and blunt accusations, after the fashion of the militant *literati* of the past, the reason of his animosity is easily explained.

Max Nordau, like many scientists before him and with him, has taken sides in the absurd fight—the *querelle allemande*—between science and religion, which has done so much to discredit both. To the unprejudiced observer, any scientist who joins in the fray is induced to do so by his inability to distinguish between religion and church, and consequently to realize that the whole progress of science during the present century has had the result, amongst many others, of justifying such an attitude of mind towards God, the original cause, universal energy, or whatever scientists choose to call it, which religion implies.

Whoever distinguishes between church and religion will at once understand that an ascendency of religious views throughout the world may be perfectly compatible with the decay of sectarian dogmas, and that therefore many phenomena which appear to indicate the decay of religious views—such as church-going, for example,—may in reality mean a deeper religious life. If we take a comprehensive view of that progress in religious views which has been accelerated by science, we shall find that church-going, the rosary, and the images of the saints, indicate the preliminary stages of a religious evolution which in its later development requires truer expressions.

So long as we have such a number of sects and

churches, many of which differ essentially, and all of which differ to some extent, it cannot affect any one's feelings to be told that church is not religion. It is this truth that science has accentuated, and the inevitable consequence has been that the churches, though they at first might have vehemently opposed certain scientific facts, and yet more certain rash speculations founded on them, they have afterwards quietly striven to modify their views and their dogmas so that they should not clash with absolute scientific truths. That many such attempts at reconciliation between science and churches have been feeble and absurd does not disprove, but confirms the existence of the above tendency. Though perhaps it would be difficult to give a true definition of religion as distinguished from church, the conception which every thinking man forms of it is probably clear enough to allow him to realize that some churches are farther from the ideal than others.

If it be true that the progress of science has been instrumental in impelling the development of churches in the direction of a future religion of ideal beauty and ideal truth, and that such a religion must necessarily be in complete harmony with scientific facts, then the animosity of science and religion is to a sound mind incomprehensible.

Yet Max Nordau unhesitatingly takes for granted that religion and science are naturally antagonistic.

He takes very seriously the assumption of the French neo-Catholics that henceforth science will have to make room for religion. Had he any sense of humour, he would not have thus betrayed how *jalousie de métier* animates him to no small extent. He mixes up science and the scientists in a most amusing manner when he compares the neglected scientist with the idolized saint, and asks, "What saintly legend is as beautiful as the life of an enquirer who spends his existence bending over the microscope?" Does our alienist aspire to go down to posterity with a halo around his head? He regrets the good old time when the Daily Press of that date said, "We live in a scientific age," when "the news of the day reported the travels and the marriages of scientists, the *feuilleton* novels contained witty allusions to Darwin, etc."

Max Nordau completely denies that there is any foundation for the assertion of the French symbolists that science has become bankrupt—that it has not fulfilled its promises to humanity. In order to refute it, he gives us the long list of scientific achievements to which scientists who militate against religion have accustomed us, beginning with spectral analysis and finishing up with instantaneous photography. He demands for science the respect and trust of humanity, not only on the ground of what science has accomplished, but also on the ground of what it will accomplish.

His faith in his mission deserves sincere admiration, and proves him to be one of those earnest enthusiasts who alone can advance humanity. But he does not see that his prophecies regarding future achievements are not science, but faith and religion —based, it is true, on reasonable grounds, but still faith and religion.

Nor does he see that his proud asseveration of the achievements of science, and his prophecy with regard to its future, do not constitute a refutation to the cry of the symbolists that science is bankrupt. The promises which the symbolists refer to, as being dishonoured by science, are not of the kind that could possibly be redeemed by the achievements referred to in Max Nordau's splendid list. They allude to promises not really made by science, but by rash and prejudiced scientists. These have over and over again proclaimed that religion had been supplanted by science, and that science could, or else soon would, explain all those mysteries which religion claimed to explain or to symbolize, such as first causes, final aims, existence or non-existence before and after death, the origin of evil, the essence of morality, and so on. Science, according to them, was not only to bring about perfect serenity in man's mind regarding himself and the universe, but to satisfy the mysterious longings and the uncontrollable emotions, either hereditary, or part of man's nature, which hitherto religion alone had satisfied. Science was also to supply rational motives for purity, morality, self-sacrifice, and all the virtues and exertions which are indispensable to the elevation of our race. Finally, science was to transform us into an ideal race, living in an ideal manner, thus substituting a terrestrial heaven for humanity for the spiritual heaven which religion promised for the individual.

Max Nordau cannot blame the scientists who made these promises; for the whole of his book shows that he is in entire sympathy with them.

There was a time when the educated world believed in the arrogant promises of the scientists; when it confidently expected that mysteries, so far unexplained, would be cleared up within a reasonable time, and that systems and speculation, which were to take the place of religion, would gradually be so amended as to become capable of fulfilling so great an object.

But the rapid scientific discoveries which followed one upon each other, far from tending to fulfil the promises of the scientists, had the effect of persuading the world that science was not going to keep any of these promises. For each mystery it unravelled revealed a series of new mysteries behind it, and the explanatory task of science grew with its own progress. In fact, while the explanations increased by simple arithmetical progression, the mysteries rose up in geometrical progression.

At the same time better schools, public lectures, and innumerable periodicals, initiated the masses into the secrets of the scientific free-masonry, and people began to perceive that what they, in their awe of science, believed to be perfect knowledge of the very essence of the world-phenomenon was only a series of acute observations, an intelligent classification, backed by arbitrary speculations and the superstitious faith in the omnipotence of science, culminating simply in a barren religion of humanity.

As to eternity and infinity of space, all that science could do was to tell the masses not to trouble their heads about them; as to causality, they were asked to regard it simply as "a form of thought which had nothing to do with the phenomena." As to morality, the religion of humanity seemed extremely untrustworthy: for the removal of all personal responsibility, and the certainty of complete annihilation after death, seemed to give the strong-minded and clever people the strongest possible inducement to make their fellow-beings tools for their own happiness. The promised earthly paradise was not only thousands of years ahead in time, but was to be constituted on principles which even a superficial knowledge of economy and sociology was bound to expose as an Inferno.

It was natural then that a great number of people, unable to climb to the height of abstract and unsatisfactory reasoning of the kind that the scientists had attained to, and whose emotional nature utterly rebelled against a progression which was intended constantly to violate their best instincts, should spurn science, which offered them no other compensation than freedom from personal responsibility.

It was not only the hollow arrogance of the scientists and the failure of science to fulfil the promises of its superstitious votaries which had created disgust with scientific atheism: the practical results of the anti-religious tendencies became alarmingly apparent; experience began to prove that the discarding of all personal responsibility did not produce the *ultra* man—*der Uebermensch*—of which the scientists claimed to be the prototypes.

Many of them had been in the habit of speaking scornfully of those selfish natures who live irreproachable lives, and who devote themselves to the promotion of the good of their fellow-men, under the impression that in a future state they would reap their reward. The atheist-scientist represented himself as a man of different metal: he was fully as moral as the religionist; he spent his life in serving humanity, well knowing that his self-control and self-sacrifice would bring him no reward; he did his duty, not induced by any mean, religious consideration, but because he was a perfect man.

The lesser mortals, those from whose ranks the symbolists are recruited, began to entertain doubts of the infallibility of these first fruits of the religion of humanity. The very arrogance of these perfect men told against them. If they disbelieved in the rewards of a future life, they were not averse from the rewards in this, and eagerly accepted the money and the distinction their works brought them. There was especially this about them : they unhesitatingly attacked that which the masses could alone rely on for moral guidance, equanimity, consolation, and encouragement — religion — while the religion of humanity was thousands of years in the future, and thus left the people a prey to mental bewilderment, doubt, and unrestrained passions. The scientist stood accused of acting like a man depriving a cripple of his only crutch, against the promise of supplying his remote descendants with better ones.

But atheism had a far worse effect on ordinary mortals, who had not to sustain a reputation as apostles of the new scientific creed. Convinced that no personal responsibility attached to them, and caring little for what would happen to the next generation, or still less to generations thousands of years hence, they tried to persuade themselves that conscience was an inherited weakness, developed by evolution, or a product of wrong religious teaching. Wishing to rise above such a weakness, they did their best to silence conscience, and to live for self-gratification. In this manner selfishness, if not Egomania, was strongly developed.

Capitalists and politicians strove to acquire wealth and power, regardless of other people's rights, of their own conscience, and of their sense of honour, so long as their dishonour was known only to themselves. Society became frivolous, and exhibited the same stigmata of degeneration noticed before in decaying commonwealths. Art became lascivious and corrupting; literature became realistic and offensive. In fact, a host of clever men who ought to have been benefactors of their race cared not to what extent they ruined and demoralized their fellow-beings so long as they safe-guarded their own health, their own future, and their social position.

The working classes being told by men, far superior to them in intellect and education, that their only chance was in their lives here on earth, and that death was annihilation, began to sympathize with violent Nihilists and Anarchists, and were less averse to risk their lives, if it were only to avenge themselves on those who deprived them of their terrestrial happiness.

But it was not only in the effect on their fellow-beings that the neo-Catholics, the symbolists, and their sympathizers all over the world, beheld the results of scientific atheism. Many of these themselves became "frightful examples" of these results. Max Nordau commits a great mistake in studying the French symbolists as authors and poets. It is as children of their times that they should be studied. He looks upon them as causes of the symbolist movement, whereas we should have regarded them as the indicators of a remarkable stage in the development of our race.

It was inevitable that the theories of the scientists should have been accepted more widely in France than in any other civilized country. In the English-speaking countries the Churches and sects had not assumed the same uncompromising attitude with regard to the mediæval doctrines as the Church of Rome. They had gradually receded from one contested point after another and many of their old forms and texts were given a more liberal interpretation. Urged on by the example of the Broad Church, the Congregationalists, and especially by the Unitarians, the clergy and the ministers ceased their opposition to any established scientific facts, though they rejected scientific speculations. The influence of the scientists in the English-speaking countries tended therefore to modernize religion, instead of bringing it into contempt.

In Germany, where the people are slow to oppose

any authority, and where they are extremely shy of their real religious opinions, scientific atheism simply encouraged the free-thinkers existing there of old, and induced a mass of young men to masquerade as free-thinkers who in reality held no opinions at all, and who were destined to become devout in their old age.

In Italy and Spain the teachings of the scientists only somewhat strengthened the hands of the Liberals, but produced no effect on the Ultramontanes. In Russia, where the nobility and the middle classes had for a long time been free-thinkers, or perhaps non-thinkers, in regard to religious questions, the religion of humanity affected only that portion of the people which was already under the influence of Nihilism, and tended to render them more reckless.

In France however, and perhaps in such countries as are directly influenced by French views—for instance, Belgium and Switzerland—circumstances were different. The atheism which broke out with the first French Revolution had begun to subside, the nobility and the upper classes were the allies of Rome partly by conviction, and partly from policy. In the country districts the *curés* had resumed their influence over the peasantry, but the labouring class in the towns was divided into two camps, the free-thinkers and the Ultramontanes;

and the difference between them was emphasized by the circumstance that the Ultramontanes were generally conservative in siding with the powers that be, while the free-thinkers were more or less extreme Republicans, Socialists, or Communists.

Such was the situation in France when the influence of the scientists on religious opinion began to make itself felt there. The materialist views were eagerly taken up by the Bohemians of Paris and by the extreme wing of the Republican Press. The upper classes read, or skimmed, the English scientists, and up to the beginning of the Franco-German war the German philosophers were much in vogue amongst the upper classes and in literary circles. In this fashion the Church of Rome had to face an attack differing widely from the French Revolution. Then the corruption, and the siding of the Church with those who were regarded as the enemies of the country, exposed it to open violence prompted by strongly roused passions. During the latter days of the Second Empire it was assailed in its dogmas with arms borrowed from scientific research and speculation. The latter attack was by far the more dangerous. The discontent with the Imperial Government did much to draw the urban working classes into the ranks of the free-thinkers, where the theories of the scientists confirmed them in their new atheism.

Parisian society had become atheistic, and the whole male population of the middle class prided themselves on their freedom from all religious prejudices. What remained of religion in France was represented by the old nobility, who had a political interest in being religious; by the peasants, who were supposed to be too stupid to grasp the new scientific truths; by old men, who had not the courage to face the grave without the consolation of religion; and by the women, to whom, it was confessed even by the most debauched *roués*, religion gave an extra charm.

When the third Republic was launched it had a strong atheistic character, and the working classes in all the cities, the sincere free-thinkers, patriots, and philanthropists hoped that, under a Republican form of government the religion of humanity of the scientists would at last have a fair trial. But they were destined to bitter disappointment. The new Republic turned out to be *bourgeois* in the worst sense of the word. Politics passed into a profession. Politicians and administrators became corrupt. Scandals multiplied. Even the Press was unable to show clean hands. Wealth became all-powerful, and the plutocrats acquired an enormous influence which they did not hesitate to use to their own advantage. Speculators and adventurers pulled the strings of the home, and especially of the colonial, policy, and in order to further private interests the indebtedness of the State was carried to such a point as to threaten the most gigantic financial catastrophe the world has ever witnessed. In the meantime the working classes and even the agriculturists naturally suffered from the result of a system of government which disregarded their interests. The proletariat of the cities grew, labour troubles became frequent, wages fell, and poverty rapidly increased.

While this growing penury invaded the homes of the working and lower middle class of a nation which has only partially realized the happiness and healthy influence flowing from decent and moral homes, scientific atheism took possession of the minds of the people, especially of the men. It urged them to make the most of their lives, and enticed them into a whirlpool of dissipation.

Scientific atheism was bound to produce a vast increase in immorality in a country like France, where the Church of Rome, in order to enhance its influence over the people, favours unhappy relations between the sexes. The clergy do all they can to estrange the sexes prior to marriage, and thus prevent pure love and love-marriages, while they encourage *mariages de convenance*. They are animated no doubt by the best intentions, but, living themselves in enforced celibacy, have no idea to what an extent they thus undermine the morality of the people.

As love counts for little in the tying of the matrimonial knot, and the *dot* counts for much, French unendowed girls stand a poor chance of ever getting married. This exclusion of an enormous number of the best women from the marriage market explains, to a large extent, the many irregular households to be met with in France. The fact that lovable and high-souled women accept the position of mistresses has largely tended to multiply mock marriages. The refusal on the part of the Church of Rome to permit divorce, and the lovelessness of the regular alliances, tend in the same direction. The sum total of all this is that a majority of Frenchwomen have to choose between an unhappy married life without love, and an immoral one with it. Those who are forced into the former in a great many cases seek consolation in an illicit *liaison*; those who drift into the latter become debauched. While thus the young, respectable, and pure-minded girls are relegated to schools and nunneries and excluded from all association with young men, among these licentious pleasure often takes the place of romantic love. Hence physically and morally unhealthy lives, absence of happiness, craving for excitement, morbid passions, pessimism, contempt for life, depraved tastes, hysteria.

Scientific atheism had however only aggravated a

state of things created by sacerdotal influence on social habits. But it was only natural that a nation, so biassed in social questions as France, should ascribe the decay of morality and of so many other virtues to the weakening of that influence which for centuries had proclaimed itself, and had been considered by the masses as the only check upon wickedness among great and small alike.

Hosts of young men who entered life, with noble aspirations to fight for high ideals, soon perceived, when left to shift for themselves, that the society around them irresistibly opposed the realization of their hopes. They found it difficult, almost impossible, to reconcile success with self-esteem, love with morality, and their poetical aspirations with their manner of living. Many, in despair of happiness and success, or in order to forget their crumbled illusions, threw themselves into a feverish quest for excitement, in which health of body and mind were jeopardized.

Awakening to the full consciousness of the depth of their fall, they could not fail to see that the social system under which they lived was largely responsible for their miseries. In looking back over their wasted lives they saw nought but shattered hopes. What they had forfeited were a happy and vigorous youth, transports of romance, the love of a pure-minded woman, a strong and active manhood, a chivalrous fight for the good, the pure, the true and the beautiful, the respect of their fellow-men, an ideal home.

The social conditions which they held responsible for their miserable career, and even for the regret they experienced, could not be laid at the door of an Emperor or a dynasty: for their country was governed by universal suffrage. Finding government, legislation, institutions, and social conditions vitiated, they had to blame Society. They found that Society was atheistic, and was deprived of the only check and guide that came within their ken—religion. They were filled with an intense longing to destroy the atheism which science had created, and to return to a belief which would re-endow Society with moral order, health, romance, love, purity, and beautiful emotions.

Science was the enemy, as, under the Empire, the priest was the enemy. To discredit it was the first essential step. When therefore the actual power of science, its actual possibilities, became popularized, and each successive scientific discovery rendered the prophecies of the superstitious scientists more and more preposterous, the French symbolists took up the cry that science was bankrupt.

CHAPTER V

SYMBOLISM AND LOGIC

THE French symbolists, and all poets and artists who move in the world of emotions, are invited by Max Nordau to "take their place at the table of science, where there is room for all." Were they to accept the invitation, how would the emotional nature of our race find expression? Would it be possible, or wise, to ignore emotions in face of the fact that our lives are essentially emotional? Or does Max Nordau push his scientific superstition to such a point as to believe that human emotions can ever be investigated by means of the lancet, the microscope, and the thermometer? In spite of his sneer at Rossetti's remark regarding his indifference as to whether the sun turned round the earth or the earth turned round the sun, he cannot fail to acknowledge that what humanity yearns for is beautiful and pleasing emotions, not scientific facts. The glorious sunshine, the balmy breeze, the radiant flowers, the inscrutable attractions of woman, her love, her esteem, her faith, the affection of children, the confidence of our fellow-beings, our trust in the good, our struggle against evil—such are the elements of life and happiness. Science acquires all its importance from being the means by which beautiful and pleasing emotions are safe-guarded, and unpleasant emotions are avoided. When science mistakes its mission, when it attempts to distort and vilify their expressions, it has become unreal and fatal.

Max Nordau wishes us to regard science—progressing as it has done by replacing old errors of our senses by new errors of our senses—as embodying all facts worth noticing, and to disregard emotions which are eternally unchangeable.

To turn our back upon emotions and to take our place at the table of science means to ignore all that is beautiful, lovable, ennobling, and hopeful, to shut our eyes to the charms of form, colour, motion, and our ears to music, and to concentrate our attention upon the repast spread on the table of science : the pleasure of discovering bacteria in human tissue, the curiosity of counting the throbs of a frog's heart after being torn from the living body, the sensation of ascertaining the effect of the gastric juices of the foot of a living rabbit inserted into a living dog's stomach.

We take no side in the question of vivisection, or any other scientific methods, but without in the least minimizing the great services rendered, and to be rendered by science to humanity, we must express our astonishment that any sound mind, knowing what scientific methods are, and must be, can seriously suggest that scientific investigation should supersede art and poetry. If we believed in degeneration, such opinions would be the first examples of it we should quote.

Poets and philosophers who deal with emotions, so to say with immaterial phenomena, impalpable to every one of our senses, but demonstrated as eternally real by their effects, must needs make use of symbols, or, to be more exact, of more symbols, vaguer symbols, and bolder symbols, than those which naturally enter into language. To deny them this right is equal to denying the mathematician the use of the letter X, which stands for unknown quantities, and which is handled by him as dexterously as if it were the most familiar object in the world. If human beings were not allowed to speak about what their imagination conjures up, what their feelings prompt, and what irresistible instincts point to, they would be brought alarmingly near to the level of the beast.

The French symbolists being poets, might not have formulated into distinct thoughts what we have said above, but they have certainly felt it all, and much more. They have felt themselves surrounded by undefined and undefinable X's of far greater moment to their lives, to their happiness, and to their best instincts, than all the known and half-known quantities of science. In attempting to give expression to their feelings and to their thoughts regarding the all-important unknown, and to evoke among their fellow-beings an interest in them, they have found themselves justified in using any means, including symbolism, for their purpose.

Max Nordau has entertained no such considerations in dealing with the French symbolists. In obedience to his professional prejudices, he looks for no other causes, no other influences, than those that can be found in the mechanism of their brains. This is all the more amazing as he over and over again recognises that external circumstances, conditions of life and habits, exercise a strong influence on the brain, or, in other words, that the mechanism which connects the *Ego* with matter may be influenced by the *Ego*. The result of his criticism presents therefore a want of fairness which to the English mind is especially objectionable.

The manner in which he pries into the private life and antecedents of Paul Verlaine, and the indelicate manner in which he refers to the personal appearance of the poet, impresses us English people as so many unfair means of giving plausibility to his conclusions. When a hunchback is good-humoured enough to make fun of his own deformity, those of gentle feelings sympathize all the more with his misfortune, and become all the more anxious not to refer to it. When a poet, in his love of truth and in his anxiety to rouse a certain emotion, makes confessions, when he instances his own sad experiences and failings, when he, so to say, throws himself into the flames on the altar of truth, we in England count it indelicate and unfair to base criticism on facts thus revealed. Had Max Nordau read Verlaine's poetry with an unbiassed mind, he could not have failed to be struck by the extent to which the poet typifies the movement going on around him : his failings, his errors, and, maybe, his bad habits —all this is the fate of millions who have been induced by the materialist tendencies of recent times to disregard personal responsibility, and who, after rejecting such guides as the nobler instincts of humanity had proffered, attempt to follow the dictates of the lower instincts and animal impulses. His terrible remorse and despair, while he is still unmoved by religion, bear witness to aspirations which the materialist would fain deny. His instinctive groping for the consolations of religion shows to what an extent he attributes his failings to an irreligious life, and that he experiences within him yearnings for a happiness which the gratification of the senses, prompted by atheism, has never afforded him.

Max Nordau would object to this expression—the gratification of his senses prompted by atheism—and would tell us that atheism ought to have implanted into Verlaine the religion of humanity, and that he should have sacrificed all his inclinations for the future happiness of his race. But, surely, it would require a good dose of hypocrisy for a man, sincerely convinced that death puts him personally beyond any consequences of his life, to persuade himself that he is practising a life-long abnegation for the good of posterity. Is it not much more likely that in so frank a nature as Verlaine's the disbelief in personal responsibility would turn him into a devil-may-care vagabond until he learned in the school of experience the dangerous mistakes of materialism? Does Max Nordau not recognise the logic and the frankness in a young man who, in the exuberance of his animal life, when convinced of personal irresponsibility, lives up to the motto of a "short life and a merry one"?

The need of love and affection—a need generally so strongly felt by all poets, Max Nordau is pleased to call eroticism, and when the poet finds that he has profaned love, implanted in his soul by God, Max Nordau fancies he has discovered in Verlaine that blending of religious fervour and morbid eroticism which, when irrational, is a sign of lunacy.

When Paul Verlaine invokes the Virgin Mary, a form of religious expression which millions of sane people indulge in daily, Max Nordau at once imagines he has discovered another trace of insanity. In order to show that we are not unfair to our alienist, we will quote one of the poems of Verlaine he refers to, and the conclusions he draws from it,—

> Et comme j'étais faible, et bien méchant encore,
> Aux mains lâches, les yeux éblouis des chemins,
> Elle baissa mes yeux, et me joignis les mains,
> Et m'enseigna les mots par lesquels on adore.

"The accents here quoted," says Max Nordau, "are well known to the clinics of psychiatry. We may compare them to the picture which Legrain gives of some of his patients. 'His speech continually reverts to God and the Virgin Mary, his cousin.' (The case in question is that of a degenerate subject who was a tramway conductor.) 'Mystical ideas complete the picture. He talks of God, of heaven, crosses himself, kneels down, and says that he is following the commandments of Christ.' (The subject under observation is a day-labourer.) 'The devil will tempt me, but I see God who guards me. I have asked of God that all people might be beautiful,' etc."

So far Max Nordau.

Because a mad tramway conductor thinks he is

cousin of the Virgin Mary, Verlaine, who symbolizes in the Virgin Mary the power that draws him towards the good, is on the road to madness! From this it follows that, if a mad tramway conductor were to believe himself the cousin of Professor Lombroso Max Nordau's quasi-worship of that authority would indicate degeneracy in Max Nordau's mind.

One of Max Nordau's characteristics is a weak or dull logical faculty, often to be observed in those who over-study for examination and in specialists fanatically inclined. Without this peculiarity he could not possibly have omitted to ask himself the question, "How about all other worshippers of Christ?" when he concludes that Verlaine's mind is degenerate because he speaks devotedly of the Virgin Mary, while a lunatic labourer says that he follows the commandments of Christ. Max Nordau does not see that in this manner he completely gives himself away, and lets us perceive that it is not the symbolist whom he considered degenerate, but the whole Christian populations of the world that have existed during two thousand years, and that still exist. Only his lack of a sense of the ridiculous, already pointed out, has prevented him from remembering that the man in his cups considers himself the only sober man of the company.

The verses which Verlaine has written in praise of a vagabond life Max Nordau holds up as a sure sign of lurking lunacy. Are then all poets who write in praise of a vagabond life degenerates? Is not the true secret of Max Nordau's conclusion to be found in the fact that he entirely misses the satire against our modern system which underlies Verlaine's and other writers' poems on this same subject? He does the same with regard to Verlaine's poem addressed to the demented king, Louis II. of Bavaria. When we behold the follies of reigning sovereigns, who are supposed to be in the full enjoyment of their faculties, making such poor use of their opportunities, degrading and ruining their people, rousing a hatred against themselves and their dynasty, or striving at low *bourgeois* aims, or even, to use Max Nordau's own expression, selling their royalty for a big cheque; when we read of the monarchs of the past, of their crimes and their meannesses, how can we wonder that the unfortunate King Louis should inspire sympathy in a poet, and that he should satirize the so-called reasonable monarchs by eulogizing the demented one?

Max Nordau makes much of that form of mental weakness which manifests itself in echolalia, or the mania of repeating for no reason the same words and the same sentences. But to deny the poet, who aims at conveying an emotion and for that purpose wishes to create a certain mood in his listeners, the use of choruses, refrains, and cadenced repetitions, he runs counter to the oldest literary tradition in the world. He would surely not object to repetitions in verses intended to be sung; and if we are right in placing poetry half way between speech and music in the list of the vehicles of thought, as we have done in a previous chapter, euphonies, musicalities of words and repetitions are both permissible and rational.

Many poetical emotions may be quickened by reminiscences from childhood; and a style of writing, or the use of words or sounds, reminding us of early days, might be the most effective methods of expression. Thus, for instance, a drowsy repetition of pleasant-sounding words may be very telling in a lullaby, even if they convey no scientific meaning, or do not contribute to the sense of the poem, and so long as they do not distort it. The examples of repetitions from degeneracy in Verlaine are chosen so unhappily as to place Max Nordau in the wrong and Verlaine in the right in the judgment of unbiassed persons; the one is a seranade, and the other is entitled, "Chevaux du Bois," in which the sensation of a child on a merry-go-round is suggested. Another is supposed to be sung by, or suggests, Pierrot Gamin, that is a young idiot. When Verlaine wishes to qualify a noun in a manner which is difficult to express in ordinary adjectives, he, like millions of his fellows, has recourse to the method of giving a new, or symbolic signification, to an old adjective, and this, according to Max Nordau, is a sign of mental degeneration. To prove his case he quotes such terms as "a narrow and vast affection," "a slow landscape," "a slack liqueur," "a gilded perfume," "a terse contour," etc. He does not seem to know that the paucity of language renders such expressions not only legitimate but extremely useful in many professions and trades, let alone poetry. Has he never heard of a warm colour, a lively tint, a cold tone, etc.? Are the French wine-growers mad when they say that wine is heavy, light, full, dead, alive, slack, round, green, angular, smooth, velvety, etc.?

We are glad to see that he recognises Verlaine's ability as a poet and does not find fault with some of his poems. Thus he says of "Chanson d'Autonne" that "there are few poems in French literature that can rival" it. While rejoicing at the fairness that Nordau here displays, we must however point out the eccentricity of his logic. He desires to warn us against degeneration, and therefore points to a poet whose degeneracy has not prevented him from writing a masterpiece of literature. It should also be noticed that the "Chanson d'Autonne," which meets with such ample praise from Max Nordau, is on the same theme which underlies other pieces of poetry quoted in his work as examples of legitimate and sane poetry.

When he does intimate that a poet might burst into song over flowers, trees, brooks, and twittering birds, but not over the sympathy he feels in his consciousness with the powers that have called them forth, simply because science has not so far been able to analyse and classify those powers, he only shows that he is illogical enough to proffer his limited view of what is poetical as an infallible standard of the poetry of the world.

Max Nordau blames Verlaine and other symbolists for dealing with moods instead of with definite ideas. But is there a single poet in the past or the present who did not largely deal in moods, and who did not labour to give the world an impression of his own feelings? Max Nordau's ideal author—Goethe—has gone further. He wrote a whole novel, "Werther's Leiden," which is little else than a lengthy description of his hero's moods.

Another symbolist, Stephane Mallarmé, who in France as well as in England enjoys a reputation as a poet, or rather as an authority on poetry, is attacked by Max Nordau in a manner which suggests other motives than fair criticism. He gibes at the symbolists and at all who consider Mallarmé a poet, because he has produced only a few original works and translations. As our alienist cannot very well put this down as a sign of degeneration, having treated those who write much as graphomaniacs, he gives us no other reasons for placing Mallarmé among the examples of degeneration than that he has "long, pointed, faun-like ears," a fact which he seems not to have noticed personally but which he has obtained, like most of his facts, from a book.

He distinctly insinuates that the admiration for Mallarmé's poetical gift indicates degeneration, especially as Mallarmé has written so little. We meet here again with a striking example of his curious logic. He imagines that he strengthens his case by quoting from Lessing, who in "Amelia Galotti" makes Conti say that Raphael would have been the greatest genius in painting, even if he had unfortunately been born without hands. From this, English readers who happen to know nothing of Lessing or Conti would conclude that either Lessing was a lunatic or that his character, Conti, was mad. But neither is the case, and the quotation consequently tells against Max Nordau. Whoever would deny that a man cannot be a poet and an authority on poetry without publishing verse must attach an extremely narrow meaning to the word poet. If Lessing, or Conti, means by the word painter, not the craftsman, but the man with the painter's soul, the symbolist may surely be allowed to call Mallarmé a poet. Has Max Nordau never met with mute poets, blind painters, and deaf musicians? One of the greatest musicians of the world composed marvellous music while stone-deaf. Now if we suppose that Beethoven had lost his hearing before he had mastered the technicalities of music, would he therefore not have remained a musician?

Max Nordau is very severe on several other symbolists and certainly does his best to represent them in an unfavourable light. In order to show that Charles Morice, the author of " La Littérature de tout à l'heure" is literally insane and a graphomaniac, he quotes Morice's rhapsodical conception of God, which he pretends to take as an exact definition in order to reduce it to twaddle. To any unprejudiced reader it is evident that Morice intended to convey by this wild attempt at description how impossible it is to define God. Max Nordau's prejudice against the French nation becomes palpable when speaking of the fact that the French language lends itself badly to blank verse and that a freer treatment of it in French poetry is a comparatively modern departure which by other countries was taken long ago. He says: " But to any one but a Frenchman, they merely make themselves ridiculous when they trumpet their painful hobbling after the nations, who are far in front of them, as an unheard-of discovery of new paths and opening up of new roads and as an advance inspired by the ideal into the dawn of the future." This gratuitous insult of a whole nation gives us a vivid insight into the working of his mind. He would not have penned a sentence of such bad taste, and so marked by the echolalia he condemns in others, had he not been prompted by feelings stronger than his judgment.

CHAPTER VI

THE LIGHT OF RUSSIA

WITH regard to the Russian novelist, Count Leo Tolstoi, Max Nordau pursues the same mode of criticism as he employed against other writers. He also aims at the same object, firstly, to show that authors suffer from mental aberration; and, secondly, that the public who read their books do not do so on account of their literary merit, but because the readers are mentally afflicted in the same way as the authors.

To prove this against Tolstoi and his admirers is no light enterprise, and Max Nordau does not acquit himself of his self-imposed task without a great deal of shuffling.

He allows nothing for Tolstoi's surroundings, the social condition of the country in which he lives, and the life he has led, but lifts him out of all that tends to interpret this ultra-Russian writer, and regards him as one who has evolved some extraordinary notions in a studio far from his native land.

He who says Russia says a great deal: for the

expression denotes a vast empire, consisting of many nationalities and races, held together by a strong pressure, which seems, like the gravitation of huge heavenly bodies, to be determined by the size of the body from which it emanates. The inclusion of so many elements does not prevent Russia from remaining a great and powerful State, provided its Government soon becomes to some extent rational. The predominant nationality is made up of genuine Russians, whose characteristics are such as to render them capable of being, according to their rulers in the immediate future, an imminent danger to Europe, or a model nation to be followed by the rest of the world.

The Russian is good-tempered, patient, loyal, generous, kind-hearted, and superstitiously religious. He is extremely emotional and dangerous when aroused. His easy-going manners, his immense self-esteem, and his intense vitality, render him an easy victim to the numerous temptations which aliens are not slow to hold out to him. He is straightforward and strongly averse from hypocrisy, and when he is convinced that duty demands from him that he should assist in filling a trench with his dead body for the artillery to pass over, or to throw a bomb at the Czar, he will do it without a murmur.

His passiveness, his loyalty, and long-suffering have been cruelly taken advantage of by a long succession of governments, chiefly consisting of aliens. In Russia the most powerful bureaucracy in the world, composed chiefly of a German element, has taken possession of the power, and holds to it in a quasi-unconscious fashion, like a bull-dog unable to relax his bite.

The Government, with such legislation as exists, has gone on for centuries with scarcely any regard for the well-being of the people, and the inevitable results are slowly but surely manifesting themselves, and point to some terrible catastrophe.

The emancipation of the serfs, from which sanguine people, unacquainted with Russian circumstances, hoped so much, shook the old institutions to their very foundations, but brought only momentary relief to the suffering people. The mir-eaters, or village usurers, have swallowed up the land of the peasants, their cattle, and their implements, and compelled large hordes of people to move about the country in search of work. Employment is scarce and labour ill paid. The tax-collectors are as implacable and the Government officials as corrupt as ever. The tendency—to be observed all over the civilized world—of dividing humanity into two classes, the wealthy and the poor, has nowhere developed to the same extent as in Russia. The rich, comparatively few in number, are becoming extremely rich, but the great mass of the people miserably poor.

Extreme poverty, intensified by the pressure of the tax-gatherer and the inhuman methods of the money-lender, have a gnawing effect on a people living in an intensely rigorous climate, in miserable villages sparsely scattered over vast monotonous plains.

The Russians being a sentimental people, it is natural that their forlorn condition should cause them to brood over their sad lives during the long and lonely winter nights, or that they should be driven to drown their consciousness in *vodka*.

Such is the stage on which alone a character like Leo Tolstoi can become intelligible.

But it is not only the powerful influences from external circumstances which give that direction to Tolstoi's mind which Max Nordau insists in interpreting as a sign of degeneracy. The mode of life and the sphere of action he has adopted, in pursuance of the large and noble traits of his character, must have been powerfully conducive to his peculiar mood and ideas. Nobody who has read his works, even if only those works Max Nordau holds to be of the smallest literary merit and fullest of signs of degeneracy, would ever conceive the idea that Tolstoi's mind was weak or distorted. But if this novelist had been driven to lunacy, it would have been extremely irrational to account for his mental aberration without considering the outward circumstances that would have produced it.

Tolstoi's sympathies were roused, as those of every noble-minded man would have been roused, by the miserable existence of a people who possess all the elements of a great nation. In Russia no such ways are open to the reformer as in free States. There is no parliament, no organized political parties, no free Press. A political career is out of the question, except in the form of a consistent toadying of those in power, and of a blind obedience to those who crush the people. Any opposition to government, or even proffered suggestions, would lead to exile in Siberia, and abruptly cut short any man's activity. Tolstoi had therefore only two courses open to him: either to expatriate himself and to thunder forth in a foreign press against the abuses of the Russian Government, unheard and unheeded by his own censor-ridden compatriots, or to adopt the line of action he did.

In the cities, where the alien element prevails, and where the scum of the Russian nation congregates, he would be out of contact with his people. His emotional nature would have revolted against the police tyranny and spying rampant in the cities, and he would soon have been landed in the clutches of the authorities. He therefore elected to live among the peasants as one of them, convinced both by his feelings and his reason that he would thus directly benefit his surroundings by his example and form that leaven by which the whole mass might in time be leavened; while his writings simultaneously appealed to those of his countrymen who read books, and those who, outside Russia, sympathize with the Russian people.

We do not pretend to know Tolstoi's secret thoughts and his ultimate hopes, but we believe it possible that he may, without being an irrational enthusiast, or even a dreamer, have reckoned on his writings and opinions reaching the highest personages in the Russian empire through being read by all the upper classes of the world. He may have hoped that, after establishing his reputation throughout the literary world, and after having become the pride of his own nation, he would one day dare to speak such words to the rulers of all the Russians as might save him and his nation.

Whatever may have been his expectations, there can be little doubt that he has met with dire disappointment, not so much in his personal career as in his hopes for his fellow-countrymen.

To the framers of paper constitutions and to theoretical revolutionists, it may seem easy to introduce a new form of government and to regenerate a nation, but, to one who, like Tolstoi, is in close contact with the masses to be regenerated, who has daily experienced all the frailty of the material he has to work with, who alone tries to swim against overwhelming currents,—to him, the uplifting of a nation or a race is a herculean task impossible to approach with the clap-trap of the modern agitator.

Tolstoi, finding that it is the *morale* of the people he has to work upon, that it is in the religious tendencies of his fellow-men that their strength lies, concludes, with the full consent of his emotional being, that religious conceptions, different from the Russian orthodox Church and from the western university theology, must be the foundation on which he has to build. What therefore is more rational than that he should plunge into religious speculation, and thus expose himself to the mistake of adopting religious views which are prompted as much by the needs of the situation, the circumstances, his own and his people's characteristics, as by logical deductions. Greater men than he — Moses, Mahomet, and others—had done so before him.

Besides, as the postulates he starts from do not spring from exact knowledge, but from faith and emotion—as all religious postulates necessarily must do,—and as these, his postulates, are diametrically opposed to those which Max Nordau would presuppose, Tolstoi's conclusions must be the opposite of his; but to differ from Max Nordau is to be degenerate.

It is no wonder then that Tolstoi's books should be more than novels. He had a higher purpose in view than gathering in royalties and entertaining his readers. His books are jam with a considerable amount of powder in them. If, despite this, they have been widely read throughout the world, ordinary minds would conclude that in creating them their author has accomplished tasks which alone a mind of a high order could hope to perform. Our alienist, determined to come to no such conclusion, supposes that all those who read Tolstoi's works are degenerates, and that the large sale of his books is consequently a confirmation of Tolstoi's degeneracy.

Would Max Nordau apply the same kind of reasoning with regard to the sale of his own works? He would probably; but instead of starting with the supposition that contemporary readers of books are incipient lunatics, he would very likely take for granted that the readers who approve of his works are highly intelligent, and that the great sale they have attained proves the soundness of his own mind.

In support of his view, Max Nordau, who fairly acknowledges the great qualities of Tolstoi as a writer of fiction, has the audacity to assert that it is not this great quality of his works that has secured him his world-wide fame, but that it is due to his mysticism, which a degenerate race prefers to a literary and moral value. The only semblance of proof he gives for this view is that Tolstoi's best works have not contributed to his reputation so much as the "Kreutzer Sonata," "an inferior creation, which in the public opinion of the western nations placed him in the first rank of living authors." But who has decided that the "Kreutzer Sonata" is inferior to Tolstoi's other works? Only Max Nordau, whose opinion runs counter to "the western nations." If therefore there is any value in Max Nordau's argument it rests entirely on the astounding fact that the "western nations" are all degenerate and Max Nordau alone is sane.

Max Nordau, like most German bookworms, evidently believes that references to an authority, however obscure, are enough to prove any assertion. He has manifestly worked with any number of "conversations-lexicons" and encyclopedias about him, in quest of some printed confirmation of the extraordinary opinion that the "Kreutzer Sonata" is a poor book, and that the preceding works of Tolstoi alone contain those grand qualities which Max Nordau recognises. He finds that Franz Bornmüller, an author of a biographical dictionary, said in 1882 of Tolstoi: "He possesses no ordinary talent for fiction, but one devoid of due artistic finish, and which is influenced by a certain one-sidedness in his views of life and history."

It should be noticed that Max Nordau gives this quotation in order to show that Tolstoi had not attained any European fame in 1882, that is, before the "Kreutzer Sonata" was written; but with that amazing want of logic characterizing his whole work, he does not see that this Franz Bornmüller thinks very little of the early works of Tolstoi. He consequently differs from Max Nordau, and shows every sign of sharing the opinion of the "western nations."

Max Nordau makes a sharp distinction between Tolstoi's novels as such and the philosophy they enforce. He is thereby enabled to give some plausibility to the sophistical assertion that it is not Tolstoi's novels, but his philosophy which brought him popularity. This philosophy, which is supposed to prove that Tolstoi's mind is not sound, Max Nordau sums up in the following way:—" The individual is nothing, the species is everything, the individual lives in order to do his fellow-creatures good; thought and inquiry are great evils; science is perdition; faith is salvation." Among these items there is only one which differs from the views of the bulk of humanity—from that ordinary common-sense which Max Nordau so often takes as a standard of sanity, even in the superstitious peasant. We refer to the item in which he says that thought and inquiry are great evils. Nowhere in Tolstoi's writings can such a nonsensical phrase be found. It is one of those little touches that Max Nordau so dexterously applies, or which his prejudice causes him to apply, in order to strengthen his case in his readers', or perhaps in his own, eyes. He appears to ignore such works as "My Confession," "My Faith," "A Short Exposition of the Gospel," and "About my Life," all works built up by elaborate thoughts. The whole life of Tolstoi has been one of "thought and inquiry," and all his literary work is an invitation to think and to inquire. Tolstoi objects only to such thought and inquiry as vainly attempt to carry the methods of inductive science into spheres where the observation of our senses is of no avail, and where their failure tempts us to believe in the non-existence of that all-important portion of the universe into which faith alone can penetrate.

That Tolstoi should distrust science, after the presumptuous attitude which scientists have taken up, will surprise nobody who has read what we have said about this bankruptcy of science. Many scientists, including Max Nordau, have in their gratuitous attacks on religion so recklessly mixed up scientific fact with scientific speculation, that they must blame themselves if people use the term "science" when it would be more correct to employ that of "unscientific speculations."

That a thinker, who is at the same time the instructor of the ignorant masses, should look upon faith as a means of salvation, is not new, and cannot be considered as a sign of mental aberration; for millions of sane common-sense men have for thousands of years held this opinion. Even if we apply the word salvation exclusively to society in general, to the race, or to one nation, leaving out any references to individual salvation in another world, faith of some kind is the only source from which it could spring. Scientists of Max Nordau's type seem unable to understand that science means the knowledge of absolute facts which, while quite capable of undermining and destroying the foundations on which a more or less primitive religion rests, cannot possibly come into collision with faith in the widest sense of the term. When a scientist and a religionist differ about things which have not come under scientific inquiry—such as the final aim of the scheme of humanity, for example—the dispute is not between science and faith, but between two different faiths. Science therefore cannot regulate our conduct, determine our views, or save a nation. This alone can be done by faith, be it based on science, on tradition, or emotion. A great scientific knowledge might be degraded into an excuse for, and a means of, an irresponsible, selfish, and wicked life; or it might ennoble the mind, intensify the sense of responsibility, and serve as the means of rendering great services to humanity. All depends on the faith of the scientist.

The end of what we may call the era of scientific atheism, now at hand, presents most deplorable results, as we have already pointed out, of removing the only foundations of a moral balance available to those who have not had any opportunity of drawing from scientific studies that strength of character, and those noble aspirations to be met with in scientists who have a genuine faith—a faith in their science and in humanity, if in nothing else. Tolstoi, who, like every thinking man of our time, had seen the disastrous effects which scientific atheism had produced, cannot possibly be regarded as of weak intellect because he rejected scientific superstition and proclaimed faith as the true basis of conduct and character.

Max Nordau finds traces of degeneracy in Tolstoi's question, "Wherefore am I alive?" and in the manner in which Tolstoi finds a reply to that question. It seems however that Max Nordau too has asked himself that question, for in his book "Degeneration" (page 149) he replies to it in a close, well-reasoned passage, which deserves to be read to its full extent. We shall quote only a part of it in order to compare the reply he himself obtains with the reply obtained by Tolstoi. After having shown that the aim of a man's life is necessarily involved in the greater question—the aim of the universe—and that such an aim cannot exist objectively in time or space, he says: "But if it is not objective, if it does not exist in time and space, it must, in order to be conceivable, exist somewhere, virtually, as idea, as a plan and design. But that which contains a design, a thought, a plan, we name consciousness; and a consciousness that can conceive a plan of the universe, and for its realization designedly uses the forces of nature, is synonymous with God. If a man however believes in a God, he loses at once the right to raise the question, 'Wherefore am I alive?' since it is in that case an insolent presumption, an effort of small, weak man to look over God's shoulder, to spy out God's plan, to aspire to the height of omniscience. But neither is it in such a case necessary, since a God without the highest wisdom cannot be conceived; and if He has devised a plan for the world, this is certain to be perfect, all its parts are in harmony, and the aim to which every co-operator, from the smallest to the greatest, will devote himself is the best conceivable. Thus man can live in complete rest and confidence in the impulses and forces implanted in him by God, because, he, in every case, fulfils a high and worthy destiny by co-operating in a, to him, unknown Divine plan of the world."

We here notice his words: "that which contains

a design, a thought, a plan, we name consciousness." Now, nobody knows better than the scientists that so far all scientific discovery has revealed plan, method and purpose, in the smallest thing and the smallest phenomena in the universe. Is it then necessary to be degenerate to believe in a self-conscious Providence? John Stuart Mill observes that the fact that we find in nature, especially in human and animal bodies, physical and mechanical problems solved in the same way as engineers had solved them long before they knew of such solutions in nature, points not only to the existence of an intelligent Creator, but to a similarity of his intelligence to that of human beings.

According to the passage from Max Nordau, then, the planning in nature proves a conscious force, a conscious force is synonymous with God, and the man who believes in God can live in complete rest in his faith. Tolstoi obtained a reply to his question in a manner which he describes in the following words:

"It was quite the same to me whether Jesus was God or not God; whether the Holy Ghost proceeded from the one or the other. It was likely neither necessary nor important for me to know how, when, and by whom the Gospels, or any one of the parables was composed, and whether they could be ascribed to Christ or not. What to me was important was that the light, which for eighteen hundred years was the light of the world is that light still; but what name was to be given to the source of this light, or what were its component parts, and by whom it was lighted, was quite indifferent to me."

The difference in the two replies is one of words only. If therefore Max Nordau acknowledged that a sensible man could ask such a question, and if the reply of Max Nordau we have just quoted is recognised by him as his own opinion, he and Tolstoi would stand very much in the same category. But Max Nordau does not think that a perfectly sane mind would ask such a question; and if it was asked, he has another reply. This reply is however far from being so clear as the other. "If," he says, "on the other hand, there is no belief in a God, it is also impossible to form a conception of the aim, for then the aim existing in consciousness only as an idea, in the absence of a universal consciousness, has no locus for existence; there is no place for it in nature." From this it ought to follow that, if a man does not believe in God, there is no God, and consequently there can be no aim. He then proceeds to argue that, if there be no aim, it is useless to ask the question: "Wherefore am I alive?" but that we can ask the question, "Why do we live?" His reply to this is characteristic: "We live in obedience to the mechanical law of causality, which requires no plan and no universal consciousness."

It is curious to behold how Max Nordau cannot perceive that his question, "Why do we live?" implies the question, "Whence the mechanical law of causality?" and that his reply is simply, "We live because we live." Once he has accepted this self-delusion as a solid foundation, his reasoning again becomes rational, and does not bear on the point before us. The most astounding part of it is that Max Nordau considers Tolstoi, and all others whose instinct, whose emotion, and whose immutable reasoning point to a cause behind Max Nordau's home-made mechanical law of causality, as thereby showing signs of mental degeneration.

Max Nordau, in order to prove the confusion existing in Tolstoi's ideas, seems to take for granted that the tendency towards Pantheism, perceptible in the Russian's reasoning, is utterly at variance with Christianity. We would simply point out that Tolstoi has his own Christianity, framed on his own interpretation of the Gospels, and not any previously existing Christianity, and is therefore at liberty to proclaim a creed which has a Pantheistic tendency without exposing himself to the reproach of being inconsequent. But we consider it more important to notice the fact that the Gospels, far from laying down any dogmas, are the record of the life of a man—divine or not divine—whose mission it was to protest against dogmas. He called God "Father," in order to speak of universal consciousness only in its relations to man, leaving it to the doctrinaires and the philosophers to agree as best they could on the question of Pantheism or no Pantheism. Besides, the Gospels certainly emphasize the omnipresence of the Creator; and if this Pantheistic tendency had not existed among the disciples, it is not likely that St. Paul would have said, "In Him we live, we move, and have our being."

The shallow, superficial manner in which Max Nordau treats Tolstoi's ethics is certainly unworthy of him, and amounts simply to a quibble. These ethics, correctly summed up, "Resist not evil, judge not, kill not," which correspond precisely with the teachings of Christ, Max Nordau does not regard as ethics, but proceeds solemnly to test them as expediencies in peculiar cases, and comes to the conclusion that they are ridiculous.

Must we then conclude that Max Nordau has no such ethics, but that he believes it right to return evil for evil,—vendetta fashion,—that he objects to suffer wrong for a good cause, and that he revels in indiscriminate murder? Tolstoi's ethics, as ethics should do, hold up the ideal for which we should strive, and as a practical test of them we must consider not the murder and plunder of one good man by a bad one, but the state which would ensue if all men conformed to them. The practical moral we ought to draw from them is not that laws and law courts should be abolished, but that laws should be framed and law courts should be managed in such a way as to favour a general acceptance of such ethics. Here again Max Nordau indulges in illogical reasoning, and in contradictions of himself. He takes for granted that humanity is so utterly depraved that if "the fear of the gallows did not prevent it, throat-cutting and stealing would be the most generally adopted trade." This means that Max Nordau in one place in his book declares human beings are too good, too noble, too honest to need any belief in a hell, but in another place declares that they are far too depraved to do without the fear of the gallows. He forgets that good ethics have sprung from the good instincts of our race, and that crime has largely been fostered by bad laws, bad law courts, and bad institutions.

In one of his stories, entitled "From the Diary of Nechljudow," Tolstoi's hero, Prince Nechljudow, is a most eccentric character, created probably for the purpose of showing the absurdity of indiscriminate charity and other impulsive actions of the erratics of our day. Max Nordau gives an account of one of the instances in which the Prince's selfish way of practising charity is forcibly brought out. He evidently does this in order that the Prince's action should be accepted as an illustration of what Tolstoi means by charity. This is both absurd and unjust. It amounts to an identification of the author with the character he represents—a way of insinuating degeneracy in authors who simply hold it up in their characters as a warning. To thus mix up authors with their characters is a mistake frequently committed by unintelligent readers, but it is surprising to find that with Max Nordau it is an habitual method.

With regard to the character Pozdnyscheff, Max Nordau does the same thing. He takes for granted that the opinions expressed by this character are those of the author. The passages he extracts from "Short Expositions," in which Tolstoi's own opinions are expressed, in no wise justify such a supposition.

Max Nordau's explanation of the enormous success Tolstoi's books have achieved is that it is due to general degeneration among the upper classes throughout the world. If he could personally meet the hundreds of thousands of English people who have read Tolstoi's works, he would be able to form an idea of the immensity of his mistake. He would find that the majority of these people belong to a middle class, consisting of persons who are not overworked and who indulge in none of the vices of the continental aristocracies. Their muscles and their nerves have been strengthened and fortified by a healthy education, and by a love of bodily exercise, sport and even danger, and by a moral life. They live in a country where the authorities have found that to proscribe any licentious book is to promote its sale, and where consequently there is hardly any check upon morbid literature. Yet there is not a country where less of it is circulated than in England. It is true that these readers of Tolstoi have not attained to that height of intellectual development which would permit them to accept Max Nordau's "mechanical causality" as a satisfying explanation of the universe; but, on the other hand, it would be difficult to find a people so religiously inclined, and yet so free from superstition and fanaticism.

Some of them may like Rossetti's pictures, and many of them Burne Jones's, but as a rule they have an equal admiration for Raphael, Tintoretto, Correggio and others. They cannot be classed among the mystics on that account. As few of them write books, they cannot be called graphomaniacs. Nor do they show any signs of being egomaniacs. Nor have they any physical stigmata of degenerates. The heads of this class are generally beautifully shaped, and the ears of the women are by all foreigners who visit this country proclaimed to be the finest and daintiest ears in the world. Personal beauty among this class is decidedly on the increase; for each generation seems to be better-looking, and the youngest is generally the most beautiful. The latter fact, we may mention, is no doubt due to the increasing tendency of the upper and middle classes in England to beautify their homes and to surround themselves with exquisite objects, as well as to a more intellectual education, pastimes, pleasures, and arts.

Why then must these readers of Tolstoi's works be classed as degenerate?

It is not denied that in England there are people who exhibit signs of mental degeneration, but they are to be found more in literary and political circles than in the close ranks of the upper and middle classes. We would not undertake to class them under the headings established by the alienist, and it would be difficult even for Max Nordau to do so. Perhaps they are not sufficiently advanced in degeneracy to be so classed. Such signs as they exhibit are some of them as old as the hills, and others are clearly the manifestations of that intellectual and moral daze which generally follows on the destruction of the religious foundations of belief involved in the acceptance of belief in scientific atheism. But the most prevalent form of degeneracy is that which is palpably the result of financial depression, felt not only in financial but artistic and literary circles. For reasons which we leave to the economists to explain, England's commerce and agriculture seem to have come to a dead-lock. The result seems to be diminished incomes all round. Many artists, *littérateurs*, and politicians are at their wits' end how to make an income, and there can be little doubt that this has fostered a certain amount of demoralization. Extraordinary attempts are made to produce sensational pictures, to write eccentric poetry, to send forth books that will shock, and to treat of risky subjects on the stage. Politicians are obliged to make politics a profession, and, as popularity is indispensable to it as a profitable profession, they worship majorities. Anyone who is acquainted with London cannot doubt for a moment that these forms of demoralization spring entirely from a necessity of making a living. Artists, authors, and politicians of this class are no more inclined to lunacy than the vast class of people who do distasteful work, as well as those who have to appear before the public in dangerous but not much esteemed performances. If the financial depression is destined to disappear, there can be little doubt that the majority of these signs of demoralization will also disappear.

There are in this country, as everywhere else, real degenerates, people who have weakened their brains and moral faculties by drink, debauch, over-work, or persons who have inherited mental debility. There are also among us, we regret to say, an alarming number of destitute people who have been driven into mental derangement by those terrible pangs that misery inflicts. But all these degenerates care as little for Tolstoi's novels as they do for Rossetti's or Burne Jones's pictures.

Though English circumstances are vastly different from continental, there can be no doubt that the causes which have rendered Tolstoi's novels popular are the same here as in other countries. The scientific atheists have introduced into literature a materialist, selfish, sceptical, pessimistic, and cynical tone which was tolerated by the public for a long time. On the continent they had Zola and his wretched imitators, whose books found their way among us, while England has produced a crop of neurotic story-tellers, playwrights and versifiers, made up for the most part of masculine women and effeminate men, who have exploited to the utmost the atheistic vein.

The noble spirit which atheism was to bring to the front somehow did not take to literature, and the reading classes of the world began to miss those pure joys which reading used to afford them. The books of the day offended their religious feelings, their sense of decency, their loftiest conceptions of the world, and their self-esteem, without amusing them. The whole literature of fiction had become stilted, and the morbid and pessimistic authors departed so widely from nature and evinced so many signs of utter insincerity that the reading world longed to be face to face with a man who spoke his innermost thoughts. The world was therefore ready for a new departure in literature.

What wonder then that Tolstoï's works were well received. They bore witness to consummate ability, a close study of human nature. They presented a true picture of social Russia. They afforded an insight into the Russian mind. His readers experienced the intellectual treat offered by few books,—that of feeling the presence of a master-mind, and of following the thoughts of a thoroughly sincere writer, free from the cheap, ready-made materialist philosophy— a man who devotes both his life and his work, with almost superhuman energy, to the regeneration of his race.

CHAPTER VII

THE REAL IBSEN

IN reading Max Nordau's chapter on Ibsen, one cannot help wondering why our alienist has given his book the form he has. The feeling which the preceding contents of his work have more or less inspired—that there is a discrepancy between the apparent plan of the work and its execution—almost ripens into conviction on the perusal of his chapter on Ibsen.

He says in his dedication to Professor Lombroso, "Now I have undertaken the work of investigating the tendencies of the fashion in art and literature, of proving that they have their source in the degeneracy of their authors, and that the enthusiasm of their admirers is for manifestations of more or less pronounced moral insanity, imbecility, and dementia." He also says that he "ventures to fill a void in your (Lombroso's) powerful system." From what he says higher up on the same page about the power of books and works of art to influence the masses, and his many hints in other parts of the book, as, for example, in its concluding pages, we must understand that his great object is to do what he can to arrest the downward movement of human intelligence.

He thus assumes that there is a degenerating process going on throughout civilization, but attentive readers of his book feel the whole time that this assumption, far from being proved to be correct, rests on data supplied by Max Nordau, which strongly warn his readers to accept them only with a grain of salt.

On the other hand, there are a host of indications in all civilized countries pointing to an increase in intellectual power, moral strength, and æsthetic refinement. Some of these indications would probably not be undervalued by Max Nordau himself: the rapid progress of science, the increasing education among the masses, the large number of newspapers and periodicals dealing intelligently with various branches of knowledge, professions, and trades, the wider application of scientific methods to industry, wonderful inventions, not the outcome of discovery, but of intelligent induction, the decay of superstition, love of investigation, etc. Max Nordau, having allowed that the test of a sound mind is its ability to attend rationally to one's business, ought to recognise that the growth of intellectual power is manifest in improved business methods, skill, manufacturing, complicated and daring financial schemes, ingenious co-operative systems, well-managed and disciplined trades unions, nay, even cleverly laid plots to defraud.

An increasing moral strength is proved by the growth of the altruistic feeling, the devotion with which the cause of humanity, morality and progress is served by people who, thanks to scientific scepticism, expect no reward in another world; the greater sincerity observable in all religious bodies, the magnitude of charitable institutions, the magnificent heroism displayed by captains and crews on sinking ships, by our life-boat men in attempting to save the shipwrecked, by our colliers' efforts to rescue the victims of explosions, etc. The great victories of the Germans over the French and the complete success of the commanders' daring tactics have been largely, and probably correctly, ascribed to the moral qualities of the German army, while the utter defeat of the French cannot be ascribed to the want of moral qualities, but to bad leadership. A quarter of a century has elapsed since the Franco-German war, but there is no reason to believe that the moral qualities of the German army have degenerated. That no degeneracy has taken place in the English, French, and Italian armies has been proved by the Chitral expedition, by the French war with Madagascar, and by the Italian operations in Africa.

If, despite these manifest signs of growing intellectual power and moral strength, Max Nordau's deep insight into psychological matters has revealed to him a mental degeneracy in the civilized world, his way of investigating such decay, his mode of dealing with it, and especially the causes he attributes to it, are too vacillating, too contradictory, and too biassed to inspire confidence. While sometimes, as in his chapter entitled "Etiology," he refers to such causes as the increase in the consumption of spirits and tobacco, the factory system, over-work, over-crowding—all causes palpable to all who have given any attention to social questions—in the rest of his book he seems to regard certain popular writers and artists as the great cause of general degeneration who should be specially noticed. This contradiction cannot be explained away on the plea that his book is only part of a wider investigation which has already been made, or might be made, regarding the causes of degeneration, and that, so long as his work is intended to treat of the influence of literature and art, his ignoring of other causes is legitimate. If an effect is first attributed to one cause and then to another, we may be sure that there is something wrong with the reasoning. We cannot prove first that the tendency to hysteria, so common in people engaged in a certain class of business, is due to over-work, and afterwards prove that the same tendency in the same people is due to Rossetti's pictures or to Swinburne's poems.

Max Nordau never furnishes an explanation of the enormous importance he attaches to the influence of writers and artists, and the small importance he attaches to the more palpable causes of degeneration, of the existence of some of which he is aware. Nor does he tell us how he reconciles the two facts, alternately insisted upon by him, that degeneration in artists is the cause of degeneration in their surroundings; and again, that the degeneration of their surroundings is the cause of degeneration in artists and authors.

If such artists and authors as Max Nordau believes to be degenerate are the effect of degeneration all round, they are surely the smallest and least deplorable results, and it was certainly not worth while to write so bulky a volume about them. Max Nordau mentions about a score; and what is a score compared to the mass of humanity, or to the five hundred million people included in western civilization? A degeneration that would not have other results than that of producing twenty degenerate men, who, though they are in many respects a source of enjoyment to many, may have a grain of insanity in their brains, would not be worth noticing. If, on the other hand, these supposed degenerates are not what, to the ordinary mind, they decidedly appear to be—the children of their time—but the actual causes of such serious psychological effects which statistics seem to reveal, we are face to face with a phenomenon which surely demanded a different method of investigation.

The real connection between the causes and the effects should have been ascertained. For instance, the most alarming feature of degeneration in England —that weak-mindedness which leads to drunkenness —should have been connected with the mystical painters and poets, and should have been proved not to have been the result of those causes which seem palpable to every man. Then the influence of individuals on the masses in general should have been ascertained. History offers a wide field for such an investigation. If it had been found that authors and artists exercise less influence than other individuals, such as sovereigns, statesmen, prophets, reformers, revolutionary leaders, discoverers, explorers, and others, the influence of these should have at first been studied, and what could not be attributed to them might have been laid at the door of artists and authors.

In examining history, old and new, we are struck with the extremely slight effects which have been produced by *littérateurs* and artists, and the enormous, all-powerful influence exercised by other individuals. Books have influenced books, poets have influenced poets, painters have influenced painters, but the political, social, intellectual, moral, and æsthetical development of a nation has over and over again been completely determined by men who have been neither artists nor authors.

In modern times the same fact is palpable. Has ever the world been influenced more than by such men as Cavour, Prince Bismarck, Mr. Gladstone, Napoleon III.? and how might not the fate of humanity be determined in the near future by such men as, for example, the Emperor of Germany and the Czar of Russia? On the mental qualities of the Emperor of Germany depends largely whether Germany is to be crushed under the army system; whether it is to be ruined by financial blunderings; whether there shall be peaceful development of its resources, or war to the knife between its classes; whether healthy reforms shall gradually clear away its social anomalies, or whether a revolution of unprecedented atrocity shall uproot its very foundations; whether its inhabitants shall develop those characteristics to which peace and happiness are conducive, or those which would inevitably be fostered if Germany were made the battle-field of modern armies.

On the mental qualities of the Czar depend directly the destiny of a hundred million people, and indirectly the peace of the world. Russia is only too willing to progress under an imperial leader. On the occasion of his accession to the throne and his marriage, millions of people anxiously scanned his portrait and tried to read in his features the fate of Europe. The presence of lines supposed to indicate weak character produced prophecies of clerical domination, opposition to progress, and death to Russia; while a kindly expression of the eyes inspired many with hopes of a new era for Tolstoi's unfortunate countrymen.

It is not only personages of high rank and sovereign power whose mental state is of utmost importance to humanity. The political situation in most countries is capable of producing at any moment a man who, without being either an author or an artist, might be able to change the destiny of nations. It is not the opportunity that is wanting, it is the men. France is panting for a man. The working classes in America and in England stand in need of a good leader. In Germany Liebknecht threatens to divide the power with the Emperor. A political Tolstoi might, at the head of the Russian people, sweep the recreant bureaucrats from his Fatherland.

It is then sovereigns, politicians, and popular leaders whose mental state is of the utmost importance, and whose influence may overwhelmingly determine the mental and moral development of humanity. An answer to the question whether they are degenerates, or whether they are of mentally or morally sound mind, is momentous to the whole civilized world, especially if it be admitted that the minds of the race are so susceptible of being moulded by the minds of influential men.

But who are the men whom Max Nordau blames for the degeneracy for which he finds the proof in statistics? Poets and artists, whose very names are known only to the educated classes, and who for the most part supply what the market demands, or simply reflect the society around them. The most surprising of all is that he himself denies any power or any talent in some of these men, calling them—to omit his worst epithets—such names as drivelling idiots, weak-minded graphomaniacs, etc.

One condition seems however necessary before a man can receive the compliment of being called names by Max Nordau—he must have attracted public attention. We have therefore said, and repeat it, that his desperate attempt to make out Ibsen to be a degenerate renders it impossible to form a clear idea of his object, or of his reasons, for the methods he has adopted.

Henrik Ibsen aims not at being a prophet, a teacher, or a regenerator of mankind either by literary or scientific methods. No one can detect in his works special ethics, or particular religious or social views. It is characteristic of his pieces—and according to many of his opponents a great fault in them—that he points no moral, that the questions involved remain at the end of the piece exactly where they were at the beginning, that his heroes and heroines are no heroes and no heroines, and cannot serve as models of conduct. His opponents and admirers alike complain that they cannot get at his meaning, and that he will not explain himself. It is therefore surprising that there should be so much talk about the influence he exercises, and that Max Nordau himself should speak about "Ibsen's dogmas," "Ibsen's code of morals," and about Ibsen himself as a "reformer."

Those who speak about Ibsen's influence on the ethics of our time cannot, as a rule, give any explanation of their meaning which can justify the importance they attach to it. They are apt to point to his influence on the English drama and blame him for certain of its objectionable features. But to those who understand his pieces it is perfectly clear that he has not been followed by English dramatists in such things as have made him famous and popular. They have contented themselves with imitating certain situations and with referring to some objectionable feature in modern society, which Ibsen does reluctantly, compelled to do so by the situation, and in order to emphasize types of character which are only too common in every civilized country, but are so closely draped in hypocrisy as to require the great dramatist's lens to show them up. His imitators

L

however exemplify entirely exceptional cases and conjure up characters the prototypes of which it would be extremely hard to find. He aims at presenting stern reality; they aim at producing risky situations. Indeed, his imitators cannot be said to have been influenced by him more than has his brilliant parodist, Mr. F. Anstey.

In Germany, as in the Scandinavian countries, complaints are sometimes raised against Ibsen's influence on women, especially young women. Our daughters are getting Ibsenized, is the cry raised by a number of Philistine parents. It is perhaps natural that Ibsen's influence on women in those countries, where the staging of Ibsen's pieces recalls more familiar presentations should be greater than in England, where the Norwegian manner of life is but little known. But too much weight might easily be attached to the difference in acquaintance with Norway. There is a far more powerful reason why Ibsen's so-called influence should appear to be more marked on German and Norwegian women than on English women.

With the exception of the United States, there is no country in the world where respectable women are better treated than in England. An old adage says, with a great deal of truth, that the wife of the German is his slave, the wife of the Frenchman is his mistress, and the wife of the Englishman is the queen of his house. The German woman certainly has of old held a position in her home which might well lead her to envy the English woman, and as the Scandinavian countries have been largely affected by Germany in their social manners and habits, the women of these countries have ample cause for dissatisfaction. Since the time of Frederika Bremer, a woman's revolt has been brewing in the Scandinavian countries, and the aspirations for more liberty, a more natural life, and more happiness, have been constantly becoming stronger, and were highly developed before Ibsen's first piece appeared. Besides, the spread of English fiction in Germany and in the northern countries of Europe has shown the women of those countries that a happier life is quite possible.

The road to the realization of such aspirations was however barred by custom and the selfish view of the question taken by the men. They had no objection to high-spirited, talented, well-dressed, and lively women, whose attractions could evoke in them romantic and ardent feelings ; and a great many knew well enough that leisure, exemption from hard work, good food, plenty of exercise, suitable friends, artistic surroundings, good books, a fair amount of pleasure, and considerate treatment, were required to transform a young woman into that feminine ideal which they worshipped in their imagination. But they repudiated entirely the idea of having such ideals in their wives. It would have clashed far too much with the traditional type of a good wife, and to marry one deviating from this type would have set the whole circle of acquaintances talking. Besides, a wife conforming to the ideal was considered an expensive luxury, leading to waste of money which could be much better employed.

Mothers of girls, well acquainted with the marriage market, consequently exerted all their energy to form their daughters for the positions they were expected to occupy. House-cleaning, washing, cooking, darning, etc., — this was what they had to learn. A demure demeanour was what they had to practise. The society of men was what they had to avoid. Romantic ideas had, above all, to be suppressed, and only such love as would come after marriage, or at least after betrothal, was considered legitimate and decent.

A great feature in their education was to closely observe the evils and troubles which followed upon poverty, and how much more comfortable life would be with a prosperous though unattractive husband than with a beloved man who might not succeed in the world. The idea of refusing a proposal of marriage from a well-to-do man, however old and prosy, was regarded as preposterous, and any respectable girl dreaming of such a thing would have been considered as a romantic, ungrateful hussy.

As the men seldom married young, the girls were taught to ask no questions about their past, and were trained to sacrifice all their ideals of purity, their dreams of love, what a free woman would call her self-respect, their future happiness, their healthful youth on the altar of Philistine respectability.

There are other ways of degrading women besides yoking them with an ox to the plough, and that they were degraded and de-naturalized the thinking German and Scandinavian women had felt long before Ibsen wrote plays. The struggle for better treatment was however extremely weak and the progress towards emancipation extremely slow. Just as oppressive government, with its police persecution, gags open discontent and drives the forces of revolt under ground, so the tyranny over the German and Scandinavian women,—when tradition and prejudice prevented open manifestations,—developed in the hearts of women, especially among the most gifted, a dangerously strong spirit of revolt.

Already at the time when Ibsen began to write there were numerous but isolated outbreaks. The old treatment, which generally resulted in turning the married woman into a dull, despondent houseslave, a soured invalid, a nagging scold, or a gossiping zany, began to produce scoffing Aspasias, neurotic adventuresses, and here and there avenging furies.

This tendency to revolt among the women was stronger in Norway than in the other countries, because it developed parallel with that ethical awakening—the new Aand[1]—which during the latter part of this century has taken possession of so many Norwegian minds; also because the strongly imaginative and comtemplative character of the Norwegian people, and the intensely emotional nature of their women, led them to brood over their wrongs in a thoroughly Norwegian fashion. Better education and wide reading tended in the same direction.

Ibsen has therefore not Ibsenized the Scandinavian ladies. He has simply seized upon a social phenomenon and, understanding its gravity, has held it up to his contemporaries for a study and a warning.

Max Nordau, having committed the egregious mistake of believing that Ibsen has invented whereas he has in reality only copied, and that a social phenomenon which is natural to intellectual and moral progress is a result of Ibsen's writings, is, in his capacity of the most German of Germans, naturally wroth with Ibsen for representing as a social evil what a normal sound-minded common-

---

[1] Aand, the Norwegian for spirit, inspiration.

sense German—the very type of the non-degenerate—would consider as a useful and comfortable arrangement. There are several excuses for Max Nordau's belief that Ibsen misrepresents reality. The improvement in woman's status in society has no doubt advanced more in Germany than in the Scandinavian countries. It is possible that the Dowager Empress's influence as an Englishwoman has not been so great as is generally supposed, but there can be little doubt that English novels, from Charlotte Brontë's "Jane Eyre" upwards, have considerably furthered justice towards German women. The close business connections between Germany and England, the numerous Germans who have had a long experience of English life, have no doubt done much to spread English social views in Germany.

The German women may therefore now have less cause for discontent and revolt than the Scandinavian women, and it is excusable if the Germans consider that they treat them fairly and well.

To observing Englishmen who visit Germany it is however clear that the whole Philistine idea of the housewife is still prevailing in that country. A great number of husbands consider it a distinct advantage to be able to throw off all restraint in their own homes and to compel their wives to accommodate themselves as well as they can to their whims, their habits, their indulgences. That exasperating type, the house-tyrant, which is found in all countries, and not seldom in England, is especially prevalent in Germany.

German men are well aware that their wives have nothing in common with the fascinating ideal woman of their imagination, and they are quite satisfied that it should be so. Their work, their studies, their profession or their business demand all their attention, and they could not dream of dismissing them from their minds when they enter their homes. A woman who would distract her husband's attention from such important subjects would be an impediment to his success, while the typical housewife, by her cares and ministrations, furthers it. Like most men, Germans have chivalrous leanings, and enjoy a courteous intercourse with ladies, but it is generally not their wives who reap the advantages of this taste. It is the other ladies, those they meet in society, and not seldom do they muster all their powers of gallantry, all their means of pleasing, and all their faculty to amuse, in the company of women of light character, often in every respect inferior to their wives.

It is those German women, who feel that their happiness and their lives have been sacrificed, not for their husbands, but to a vicious conception of married life, who sympathize with the women of Ibsen, and have thus contributed largely to the fame of that dramatist in Germany.

Ibsen has not Ibsenized the German ladies, but his pieces have revealed the existence of a grudge long harboured by German women.

It is only just to record that, though Englishwomen, especially those who live and are treated up to the English ideal, as we mentioned before, live under much happier circumstances as children, girls, *fiancées*, and wives, there are many of our countrywomen whose marriages have been a cruel disillusion. Many Englishmen marry too young, before they know their own minds, and under the feverish impulse of a first love. When such young husbands are thoughtless, selfish, or when they have made a bad choice, a miserable married life is the result. In a great number of young households happiness prevails, thanks to the strong-mindedness and tact of the young wife, who can take care of herself and of her husband also. But thousands of marriages turn out utter failures, not for want of love, but from the husband's utter ignorance of how to take care of his wife's health, beauty, and happiness.

Though it is the fashion in this country not to adapt but to translate literally Ibsen's pieces, there would be no difficulty to so adapt them as to render them exact representations of the state of many an English home. And this is sufficient to explain his fame in England. Here, as on the Continent, it is the selfish, mean, bullying husbands, who cannot find any sense in Ibsen's pieces, and who are extremely shocked at what they consider Ibsen's perversion in attempting to enlist, by inexplicable devices, the sympathies of the audience for the erring wife, when these should be vouchsafed to the husband, who appears to be such a respectable, common-sense man.

When Ibsen thus calls attention to the importance and the gravity of the feeling of revolt which has long rankled in the minds of thinking women all over the world, and which manifested itself long before Ibsen's pieces were known outside Norway, he cannot fairly be said to be responsible for the growing discontent. In reality, he has rendered the world a great service: for the new views and aspirations of modern educated women can neither be suppressed nor ignored without considerable danger to society.

In order to understand that the demand for the purification of marriage is not a transitory whim, it will suffice to consider who made the marriage laws, and, what is more important, who inaugurated the traditional views concerning them? Men alone did. Not the young men, who would be largely swayed by the yearning for true love and by chivalrous considerations, but the law-makers of old; that is to say, elderly men of influence and fortune. In the olden times, when the foundations of social customs were laid, the rights of women were considerably less respected than in our days; and under such circumstances the law-makers did not feel called upon to consider woman to any large extent, but made laws, and introduced customs, which suited themselves. What they wanted was, firstly, to marry young and beautiful wives, despite all objections that might be raised against their age, their looks, or their characters, and without much troublesome courtship; and, secondly, to keep their young wives in subjection by sheer force and legal compulsion.

It is not reasonable to suppose that the fair sex should submit for ever to such treatment, and, as the women in the English-speaking countries have already gained large concessions, it is natural that their sisters in the rest of the civilized world should struggle for reform.

It is therefore difficult to see why Max Nordau should consider Ibsen's influence so dangerous to society as to deem it necessary to hold him up as a degenerate. The enigma becomes more puzzling when we find that Max Nordau frankly allows that Ibsen has great merits and great talents. He says, for instance: "Henrik Ibsen is a poet of great verve and power." "He has the gift of depicting in an exceptionally life-like and impressive manner that which has excited his feelings." "He has the capacity for imagining situations in which the characters are forced to turn inside out their inmost nature, in which abstract ideas transform themselves into deeds, and moods of opinion and of feeling, imperceptible to the senses but potent as causes, are made patent to sight and hearing in attitudes and gestures, in the play of feature and in words." "He knows how to group events into living frescoes possessing the charm of significant pictures . . . not like Wagner, with strange costumes and properties, architectural splendour, mechanical magic, gods and fabulous beasts, but with penetrating vision into the background of souls and the conditions of humanity." . . . "But he does not allow the imagination of the spectator to run riot in mere spectacles; he forces them into moods, he binds them by his spell in circles of ideas, through the pictures which he unrolls before them." "The power with which Ibsen, in a few rapid strokes, sketches a situation, an emotion, a dim-lit depth of the soul, is very much higher than his skill, so much extolled, of foreshortening in time" . . . "Each of the terse words which suffice him has something of the nature of a peep-hole, through which limitless vistas are obtained. The plays of all peoples of all ages have few situations at once so perfectly simple and so irresistibly affecting."

Further on he again says: "It must be acknowledged that Ibsen has created some characters possessing a truth to life and a completeness such as are not to be met with in any poet since Shakespeare . . . None the less no poet since the illustrious Spanish master (Cervantes) has succeeded in creating such an embodiment of plain, jolly, healthy common-sense, of practical tact without anxiety as to things eternal, and of honest fulfilment of all proximate, obvious duties without a suspicion of higher moral obligations, as this Gina. . . . Hjalmar also is a perfect creation, in which Ibsen has not once succumbed to the cogent temptation to exaggerate, but has exercised most entrancingly that 'self-restraint' in every word which, as Goethe says, 'reveals the master.'"

We have quoted somewhat lengthily from this eulogy of Ibsen in order to render justice both to him and to Max Nordau. There is no passage in Max Nordau's book which displays more insight into dramatic art and a more intelligent appreciation of some of the subtle but marvellous merits of Ibsen's plays. We should not have thought it possible that so keen an appreciation could have been formed without seeing Ibsen's pieces acted in the original language. This eulogy becomes all the more valuable when we remember that it emanates from one of Ibsen's opponents—from a man who would fain restrain Ibsen from writing at all, and who evidently has not paid any attention to the slow but important social struggle which Ibsen so frequently illustrates.

Most people who have read these and other acknowledgments on the part of Max Nordau of Ibsen's talent, will be struck with the reckless manner in which Max Nordau defeats his own object. He wishes to warn the world against "degenerates" of Ibsen's type, and at the same time praises him as few writers have been praised, seemingly without considering that in this manner he inspires thousands of young writers with the ambition to be degenerates as Ibsen is.

To the average reader Max Nordau suggests the idea of the impossibility of reconciling so much power, genius, talent, and craftsmanship with decayed mental faculties. This all the more as Ibsen's pieces are financial successes, and he consequently shows a solid capacity for the management of his own affairs, which, as Max Nordau has already told us, and every alienist would tell us, is the safest test of a sound brain. The conclusion seems inevitable that Max Nordau is either utterly wrong when he sees all these merits in Ibsen's work, or else when he considers him to be degenerate.

In examining the grounds on which Max Nordau strives to establish his theory of degeneracy we shall no doubt find that the latter alternative is the true one.

Max Nordau first impeaches Ibsen's reputation for realism, but takes this term in its most literal sense.

The stage has its limitations, and the dramatist must have a certain licence in the creating of his situations. Ibsen is not called a realist because all that he represents on the stage is in closer conformity with reality than the representations of practically any other dramatist ever were, but because his characters, besides being individually true to nature, are types—strongly coloured types, it may be—but not too strongly coloured to be understood by an average audience. In a piece not intended to be played the characters may be more delicately moulded, but when they are to be grasped in a few flashes before the footlights they must, like the statue intended for an elevated position, be hewn in bold proportions.

In order to show how unreal Ibsen is, Max Nordau asks whether it is probable that the joiner, Engstrand (in "Ghosts"), wishing to open a tavern for sailors, should call upon his own daughter to be the odalisque of his "establishment"? By using the word odalisque, and by placing the word establishment between inverted commas, he gives a distorted idea of the tavern Engstrand is going to open. It is a question of a real tavern, not of an "establishment." Girls in similar taverns in Norway are of course exposed to temptations and sometimes to insults, but they are by no means necessarily unchaste. In selecting the employment in the tavern, Ibsen succeeds in giving an insight into the Philistine character of Engstrand, who for the sake of money would risk his daughter's reputation, but who could always fall back on the excuse that he did not intend to ruin her.

Max Nordau may be right when he says that no Paris doctor would have told Oswald Alving in "Ghosts" that he had softening of the brain. But Ibsen does not say "softening of the brain"; he makes Alving say "a kind of softening of the brain," an expression which might very well be Oswald's interpretation of what the doctor had told him in very guarded words. Moreover it is not as an alienist that Ibsen has gained his fame; it is as a dramatist.

Max Nordau quotes as another example of unreality, the sense in which the term "society" is used by the characters in the "Pillars of Society." This is an error into which Max Nordau has evidently been led by reading a bad German translation of the piece. Ibsen's characters do not mean "social edifice," as Max Nordau pedantically will have it, but the well-to-do people in the community.

Again, he thinks that excuse very unreal which Berneck gives to his foreman, whom he has not taken into his confidence. But this unreality is precisely what Ibsen wishes the public to see, and he has evidently not accentuated the unreality sufficiently, as this has escaped even Max Nordau. Max Nordau does not find the speech of Pastor Rörlund realistic enough. The fact is that the speech is a delightful parody, in no way exaggerated, of those addresses which toadying sycophants all the world over are in the habit of delivering to a magnate whom they desire to propitiate. Any one who has heard such a speech in Norway will be amusedly surprised by its comic realism.

It would be tiresome to go minutely into the proofs of unreality Max Nordau finds in Ibsen's pieces, and the bare mention of the following examples will suffice to show the futility of his attempt. He considers it impossible for a man of forty-three to inspire love, and this in Norway, where people develop and ripen so slowly. He thinks it unreal for an excitable girl to describe as a storm on the sea the passion which induces her to encourage her rival's suicide, and then when the rival is out of the way patiently to devote a year and a half to gaining the love for which her sin was committed. Our alienist, who displays throughout his book an utter lack of the sense of the ridiculous, finds the scene between Ellida, Wangel, and the Stranger in " The Lady from the Sea" ridiculous, a scene which thousands of audiences have followed in breathless silence and with deep emotion.

The puzzle is why Max Nordau is so anxious to

show that Ibsen is not a realist, and how his not being a realist can possibly be construed into an argument in favour of his insanity. Are then all the people who, as a matter of taste or as a matter of business, supply the public with unrealistic dramas to be considered more or less demented? If this is the case, what becomes of the mental sanity of Max Nordau's great model, Goethe, the author of the intensely unreal "Faust"?

Referring to the theory of heredity, frequently alluded to in Ibsen's works, Max Nordau says he cannot preserve his gravity when Ibsen displays his scientific or medical knowledge. Here again we are tempted to refer to the sandal-maker and the sandal-strings; but there is actually no occasion to do so, because Ibsen displaying his medical knowledge is a picture conjured up by Max Nordau's own imagination. We do not know what Ibsen does in his private life, but in his dramatic works he does not display his medical knowledge. What suits Max Nordau's purpose to give as Ibsen's opinions are the opinions of his characters, who, being true to nature, speak as their prototypes in reality speak. It suits Ibsen's dramatic purposes to make use of certain views on heredity, and he is all the more entitled to do so as such opinions are very prevalent nowadays, and not without exercising a considerable influence on people's minds. Ibsen may have exactly the same opinion as his characters give expression to, or he may think the very opposite, but those who thoroughly understand Ibsen's method will be convinced that he would not commit the mistake, so common among dramatists, of allowing his characters to reflect the author's personality. When Regina, in "Ghosts," in reply to Mrs. Alving, who is harping on heredity, says, "What must be, must be . . . I take after my mother I dare say," she does not express Ibsen's opinion about heredity, but that fatalistic notion which is unfortunately extremely common among women, especially when in trouble or at fault, and a reference to her mother is only a confirmation of her fatalistic belief, at which she clutches that she may rid herself of her responsibility.

If we must look for a tendency in Ibsen's works, it might be found in his attempt to show up this generally prevailing weakness in will and character which Max Nordau himself finds everywhere and which he calls degeneration. Regina, as well as Oswald, are, "frightful examples," of this weakness, and, in placing them on the stage, Ibsen has the same object as Max Nordau, namely, to exhibit a deplorable defect in modern society. Ibsen may therefore be looked upon as Max Nordau's co-operator, and even precursor, because Ibsen's characters are types of that very degeneration which

Max Nordau desires to combat. In fact, the importance that our alienist attaches to Ibsen's characters suggests the idea that if there were no Ibsen, there would be no Max Nordau. By the aid of an extremely confused and distorted reasoning, he condemns Ibsen for that very weakness which he, like Max Nordau, has discovered in modern society and incarnated in his characters as a warning to his contemporaries.

If we had not a strong objection to the *tu quoque* argument, and were not resolved to avoid it, we could here say a great deal about Max Nordau's condemnation of Ibsen's supposed illogical references to heredity, while Max Nordau himself yields to the temptation of using the absurdest logic in order to discover supposed proofs in favour of his own pet theories.

Even supposing that Ibsen did believe in heredity, is he not in harmony with his time? One does not require to be an alienist or a biologist to understand that the Darwinian theory of evolution is the theory of heredity; and one does not require to be very old to have observed that the characteristics of parents often repeat themselves in their children. In his criticism of Ibsen, Max Nordau seems to go too far when he casts discredit on the theory of heredity, with regard to which he himself goes to an extreme, when he attributes to heredity the lurking belief in a personal God in the inmost recesses of the consciousness of certain scientists. The manner in which he refers to little Hedwig's blindness will certainly induce his readers to infer that he himself does not believe in cases of hereditary blindness—an affliction which has however come within the knowledge of many. Max Nordau, in his purposeless eagerness to tear Ibsen down from his pedestal, seems to imagine that he would further his object if he could show that Ibsen is influenced by the religion of his childhood, of his youth, and of his country. To be influenced by such religion has been the case with many sane people of strong mind, especially in countries where the morality implanted in young children is based entirely on religious instruction. Even when a man ceases to believe literally all that has been taught him, it is natural that his religious thoughts should mould themselves on the early impressions, which then become symbols instead of fact. This is especially natural with people whose walk in life has precluded them from giving that absorbing attention to psychology and biology which to a sound mind is indispensable before it can master, or believe, the scientists' theories of "mechanical causality," and the annihilation of the conscious *Ego*. Max Nordau, like many other scientific enthusiasts, seems to labour under the impression that all the loud-voiced people, who affect complete irreligiosity, and who pose as free-thinkers, are really convinced that the scientific discovery of yesterday, which might be upset by the discovery of to-morrow, sufficiently explains the world and themselves. This is far from being the case. How often when we scratch the atheist do we not find the superstitiously devout. How many men could be found in the world who are so capable of satisfying all their curiosity regarding the unknown by scientific theories that they might be quoted in support of the artificiality of religious instincts? They would certainly number very few. And yet scientists of Max Nordau's stamp are apt to regard such men as the only really sane ones, and the rest of humanity as to some extent degenerate.

But how does Max Nordau know anything about Ibsen's religious opinions? He simply studies the characters in Ibsen's pieces and takes for granted that Ibsen must necessarily hold the same opinions as his characters. This absurd assumption, indispensible to his purpose, leads him sometimes into ridiculous dilemmas from which he escapes in a not less ridiculous manner. When he finds that Ibsen has *dramatis personæ* of diametrically opposed opinions and beliefs, he does not know which of them represents Ibsen's opinions and Ibsen's beliefs. Determined not to notice the simple fact that none of them represent Ibsen's views, he falls back on the expediency of declaring that, because his characters differ, Ibsen does not know his own mind, a fact which in our alienist's view points to degeneracy.

He quotes copiously from Ibsen's pieces in order to show that those characters who have committed evil deeds, without having resigned themselves to being utterly bad, yearn for confession. From this we must conclude that Max Nordau considers a longing for confession in those who have sinned as an obsession and as pertaining to stigmata of degeneration. To make capital out of this, Max Nordau sticks hard to his assumption that Ibsen's object is to preach some kind of creed by proclaiming his own opinions through his characters. Few people in the world really know what Ibsen's final object and real aims are; but his immediate object, it will be granted, is to show his contemporaries what they really are, and so sternly and so cogently does he pursue this object that, while other dramatists show their spectators the defects of others, Ibsen lays bare their own.

In showing sinners' yearnings for confession, Ibsen could not therefore be wrong unless a longing for confession in sinners is unreal or unusual, Far from being unusual, we find it in almost every human being, from the innocent child down to the brutal criminal. The police and law-court reports in England frequently relate cases in which men and women confess crimes which would never have been discovered, simply to satisfy a conscience yearning for confession. We have nothing to do here with the question as to whether this first step towards a better life is longed for in obedience to an instinct implanted in the emotional nature of man by a Creator, or whether it is the consequence of an inherited tendency originated by religious teaching and moral civil laws. We have only to deal with the fact that the conscience of all evil-doers, and especially of those who are willing to abandon evil and return to good, prompts them to confess. Max Nordau has only to consult a Catholic priest in order to learn how strong and general this yearning is.

It must also be remembered that confession, if not to priests yet to God, is part of the Lutheran creed prevailing in Norway, and that consequently confession is regarded by the people as the test of true repentance. Though auricular confession is not a sacrament in the Lutheran Church, the Norwegian ministers could tell Max Nordau how often sinners and criminals ease their consciences by confessing to them. It is hardly possible to write a serious dramatic piece without representing a struggle between good and evil. And how then could Ibsen write dramas, true to Norwegian life, without instancing that yearning for confession which is the outward sign of the inward struggle between good and evil?

Max Nordau instances the French assassin Avinain, who before being guillotined gave out as his life's motto "Never confess" as an example of a strong and healthy mind—or, at least, he regards this motto as one which only a strong and healthy mind can follow. On the other hand, he regards confessing men as men "in whom the mechanism of inhibition is always disordered, and who therefore cannot escape from the impulse to confess when anything of an absorbing or exciting character exists in their consciousness."

In this comparison Max Nordau omits the chief factor—the religious opinion, or the philosophy which necessarily determines whether the confession is a sign of strength or weakness. If the murderer Avinain was a confirmed atheist, and if his emotional nature was such as to glorify murder, then he had no impulse to confess, and consequently required no strength of mind to resist confession. If the man who glories in what is good—or, to use an expression of Max Nordau's, who has social instincts, and consequently believes that confession is his duty and an heroic action—should shun the ordeal and prefer to spend the rest of his life as a self-despising hypocrite, this would be weak-mindedness. Of course Max Nordau may always argue that to believe in the good and in personal responsibility is in itself a sign of degeneration. But this would be simply to place the question on another plane, where we have already discussed it.

What is said here about confession applies equally to what Max Nordau says about redemption. It is not, as he states, an obsession of Ibsen's, but a symbol very natural to a people of strong religious feelings. His characters could not possibly express their ideas and their emotions in any other way than that in which they have been in the habit of thinking all their lives.

Max Nordau cannot rid himself of the obsession that the dramatist must necessarily take a side in the squabble between religion and science, and between the devotees of different social panaceas, and seems exasperated because he cannot get at Ibsen's real opinion on such questions. When he persists in his egregious error of taking the opinions of Ibsen's characters as those of Ibsen, his mind gets into a maze, which leads him to the conclusion that it is Ibsen's mind, not his own, that has got into a confused state. It is very common to find a man, who by dint of study or by natural talent, has become an authority on one subject, so far losing his power of self-criticism as to believe himself a universal genius, capable of dogmatizing on every subject under the sun. It is this conceit that induces successful men to imagine that their natural specialty is not that one which has rendered them famous, but some other specialty for which in reality they have no aptitude whatever. A successful comedian believes himself to be hardly dealt with because he is not acknowledged as a tragedian. A musician considers himself an authority on the drama. The poet thinks he ought to have been a politician. Biologists imagine they would shine as social reformers.

It is because Ibsen has not yielded to this weakness, because he has not the conceit to lay down the law on questions outside his own province, but simply aspires to be a dramatist, that Max Nordau complains so bitterly of Ibsen's omission to express a distinct opinion on all sorts of subjects on which Max Nordau burns to break a lance with him. He tilts against the opinions expressed by Ibsen's characters with the wasted fury of Don Quixote attacking windmills.

We are at a loss to account for the contradictions of which Max Nordau appears to be guilty. Much of what he says in the latter part of his essay on Ibsen is in direct contradiction to what he says in the earlier part, where his praise of Ibsen's talents and abilities is conspicuous. We will give an example of what we mean. He says at the beginning of his chapter, "Each of the terse words which suffice him (Ibsen) has something of the nature of a peep-hole, through which limitless vistas are obtained." Towards the end of it he says: "Thus Ibsen's drama is like a kaleidoscope in a sixpenny bazaar. When one looks through the peep-hole, one sees at each shaking of the cardboard tube new and parti-coloured combinations. Children are amused at this toy, but adults know that it contains only splinters of coloured glass, always the same, inserted haphazard and united into mystical figures by three bits of looking-glass, and they soon tire of the expressionless arabesque."

Can this contradiction be the result of his great trust in authorities, and has he made use of two that clash, or does he write for writing's sake, differently each day according to the mood he happens to be in?

When Ibsen's characters give expression to their yearnings for greater personal liberty, for a revolt against social traditions which threaten to wreck their lives, and which they have beheld wrecking the lives of hundreds around them, they are intended by the dramatist to show what is going on in modern society. Max Nordau of course concludes that Ibsen is an egomaniac who resents any bonds on his worst instincts. Supposing that Ibsen shares personally that same longing for more individual freedom which Max Nordau so warmly deprecates, it is evident that they differ simply because Max Nordau starts from the supposition that men's instincts are necessarily bad, and Ibsen from the supposition that they are good.

The fundamental difference in opinion mainly springs from the different circumstances amongst which the two men have been born and brought up. The German, who has all his life been impressed with the necessity of officialism and police government, who has lived under the impression that his castle would be attacked by a lower caste when free to follow its inclinations, would naturally attach great importance to existing institutions. If he at the same time be illogical enough to sap at the root of that great order-producing institution—religion—and beholds that this safe-guard is becoming more and more unreliable, he naturally looks for something to take its place.

The German social system, so unjust to the working classes, has naturally embittered the people and enlisted a number of working men into the revolutionary parties, and this growing army of so-called enemies to society naturally alarms the German middle-class man and prejudices him against the proletariat. Passions and destructive instincts, instilled by long suffering, he is apt to regard as human nature from which the worst must be expected. This explains many of Max Nordau's contradictions. He wishes to abolish religion because its abolition would glorify science, but he wishes to retain the marriage laws because he fears that without them an unspeakable state of immorality would ensue. He denies a divine plan in creation which might account for the moral instinct in man, but he does not believe that morality has sprung from the only remaining source, namely, man's experience of the advantages of morality. His habit of bowing to authorities causes him to believe that morality and a pure family life are the result of the marriage laws, and not that the marriage laws are the result of man's love of morality and of a pure family life.

The Norwegian is born and brought up in a country where liberty has been the basis and safeguard of moral order; where few police are found in the cities, and where, throughout vast tracts of country, man's good instincts are the only police; where the peasant and working-classes have no desire or intention to attack the wealthy; where the people are religious because they are honest and not honest because they are religious; where self-esteem and justice would take the place of religion were it to crumble. The Norwegian has noticed that the poor are more generous than the rich, that the people are more honest than their officials, that the free man and woman are more moral than the tied ones, and that liberty elevates and oppressive laws degrade. If the Norwegian seems to attach little importance to legal marriage, it is because, in cleansing it from mercenary considerations and other low motives, he hopes to base it on such foundations as moral instinct, love, self-respect, honour, and possibly on religious belief, and thereby make it a life-long reality. It is not to gratify low instincts and licentious passions, as Max Nordau would have it, that he wishes for reform. He may be mistaken in his motives, but this is no excuse for attributing vile motives to him.

Max Nordau is not the only one who is puzzled by the many peculiarities of Ibsen's plays. Like him, many English theatre-goers wonder why his best types and his leading characters, as a rule, are so void of nobility, fine feeling, and high principles; why he always places his scenes in small towns, and not among the romantically wild country and the picturesque peasants, as Björnsen and Jonas Lie have often done; why he represents the so-called respectable and official classes in so unfavourable a light; why his women seem to be morally and intellectually superior to his men.

In order to elucidate these questions and many other peculiarities in Ibsen's plays and characters, as well as some of the reasons why a German critic should disapprove of Ibsen, it should be remembered that in Norway two cultures have met and struggled — the German and Scandinavian — but have not blended.

Of the Scandinavian nations, the Norwegians may be considered as the extreme type. While they differ from the Danes and Swedes considerably, they differ still more from the Germans. Their characteristics arise not only from race, but largely from surroundings and modes of life. The genuine Norwegian people have of old lived scattered over a vast area of country, separated by high fjells, and broad fjords, foaming torrents and dense woods, only sparingly communicating with each other, and still less with strangers, and hearing little of the outside world, they have grown into a silent, thinking, and deep-feeling nation. They have inherited from the old Viking times an unquenchable love of liberty, and all their institutions, their customs, their principles, have developed in freedom, and such virtues as they have and of which they are most proud, are the outcome of personal independence. Accustomed to personal danger on the snow-clad mountain-paths, in the vast forests, and in small open boats upon the stormy fjords, they have acquired an extraordinary degree of self-reliance. Unused to, and distrustful of, foreign ways, and seldom successful in foreign countries, they harbour an intense love of Norway and for anything Norwegian;

and while they may conceitedly think that everything that is Norwegian is great and noble, they certainly endeavour to put a stamp of nobility and greatness on everything that is Norwegian. They are proud, generous, loyal, hospitable, and can never be persuaded that lowly circumstances or poverty could possibly be an excuse for an unroyal conduct.

Born and bred amid snow-capped mountains, deep valleys, perpendicular rocks, a jagged, stormy coast —the whole wearing an air of solemn and lonely grandeur — the Norwegians are a meditative and highly imaginative people. The stirring natural phenomena peculiar to the country cannot fail to stimulate their imagination. The snow-storms, the ice-avalanches, the light summer nights, the brilliant moonlight diffused over the abrupt mountains, the dark forests and the glittering fjords, the raging storms from the Atlantic, the flaming midnight winter skies, the sunsets which so wondrously illumine the whole coast-line — such scenes, such pictures, sink into their minds and quicken their emotions.

What wonder, then, if they are full of folk-lore and the supernatural has for them an irresistible charm? They are superstitious, and believe that their actions and lives are influenced by gnomes, fairies, and trolls. Old heathen ceremonies for the propitiation of the spirits are still in vogue. They are deeply moved by music and poetry, and have a strong predilection for all that is heroic and great.

It is not surprising that in German translations of Norwegian writings—for which Max Nordau blames Ibsen's degeneracy—adjectives should have taken a new meaning; for in Norway they have been influenced by Nature's grandeur. When Norwegians say "great," they mean great as the fjeld, great as the boundless ocean; when they say "silent," they mean silent as the wood in the short summer night. Consequently, when a man, an action, a thing, is described to them, they are apt to measure it by the standard of nature's extremes around them. They are always disappointed when they behold the wonders of civilization described to them as great and wonderful. They would call the ruins of the Coliseum mean, and think no more of the pyramids than of ant-hills. Their ideas of a great man could probably never be realized, and their wonder is considerable at finding the mighty lords of England so unlike demi-gods.

It was the Hanseatic League that brought this stern and haughty people into contact with German culture. This remarkable federation of enterprising German merchants discovered that profits could be made out of the rough products of Norway, and they founded a German colony in Bergen, which rose to considerable importance. German traders gradually settled in all the other important Norwegian centres, and the whole commercial life of Norway became more or less Germanized.

At the time Germany was far ahead of Norway in everything appertaining to industry, and was already then bent on doing business with foreign countries by offering them a mass of German manufactured goods of attractive appearance, but of little value, and not indispensable to a people like the Norwegians. Competition was already severe in Germany, money had acquired an immense importance, success in life was most easily attained by intense application to business, saving, and grinding. The German traders stood in the same relation to the Norwegians as that in which English traders stand to the native races whom they first approach for business purposes. The traders and agents who went as far as Norway—a long distance before the days of steamers and railways — were daring and reckless men, bent upon making money just as the pioneers of British commerce were and are in Africa. What interested them was not the great and noble aspect of the Norwegian character, but the desire on the part of these people to buy gew-gaws, and the facility with which they parted with their money and their goods.

Though Norway is a poor country, it yielded

to the not over-ambitious Germans a satisfactory harvest, and a great number of them settled permanently in the Norwegian towns. They became sufficiently numerous and influential to impress a German stamp on Norwegian urban life, on the people who worked and lived with them; and these became Germanized to no small extent.

These middle-class Germans were no doubt excellent, respectable people in their way, but they had little in common with the Norwegian country folk. They were better educated, they had more worldly wisdom, their experience in their own cities had trained them to subject their emotional nature to their intellect. In order to push on to success in their German communities, where antagonistic and powerful magnates left but little scope for daring and straightforwardness, they had learned to value diplomacy and discretion.

They had no sympathies with the natives, whom they regarded as semi-barbarians, and all their intercourse with them was diplomatic and insincere, and their sole motive was profit. The honesty, the pride, the generosity of the Norwegian peasantry were well known to them, but they took advantage of these characteristics, which they regarded as expensive luxuries.

The cities however became the seats of the educational establishments, and the Norwegian youth who were intended for the professions came to the cities and mingled there with the German element. On the other hand, the sons of the citizens went into the country in professional capacities and created there a middle-class strongly impregnated with German culture. In this manner a sharp line of demarcation arose between the upper and middle class on the one hand and the peasantry on the other, the former being strongly influenced by German culture, the latter clinging tenaciously to the Norwegian.

It is no slur on the German character and German culture to say that it involved degeneration in no small degree. It partook of the drawbacks of our civilization, and what happened in Norway has happened in every country where modern civilization has come into contact with nations whose virtues and noble qualities have rested as much on ignorance and the absence of temptation as on inborn worth. Thanks to the historical development we have indicated, the Norwegian upper middle classes, as well as the whole of the urban populations, developed characteristics which drew upon them the contempt of the peasants. Their eagerness for profit, their love of money, their indifference to the great, the noble, and the beautiful, their cringing attitude towards authorities and towards the wealthy, their sacrifice of public interests to private welfare, their susceptibility to the influence of foreign fashion, manners, and vices, all this tended to lower the upper and middle classes in the eyes of the peasants.

When the phenomenon, witnessed in all civilized countries—the impoverishment of the masses—made its appearance, public-spirited men began to inquire as to the causes. It was in the middle of this century, when a spirit of revolution and reform was abroad, that the yearning for a better state of things began to manifest itself. There were no aristocracy, no established Church, and no privileged class to blame for the unsatisfactory state of the country, and consequently the investigators turned their attention to the ethical condition of the people themselves. Comparison between the olden and the modern times was instituted. The discrepancy between the two classes became striking, and the corrupting influences were traced to the towns. A strong desire to revive and strengthen the old culture took possession of many men and women, who, though educated, had a keen sympathy with the peasants. To found the future development of Norway on the basis of the old Norwegian culture became the object of a new national party, including some of the best elements of the Norwegian nation. These enthusiasts found their expression in composers like Tjerulf, and in the writings of men like Björnstjerne Björnsen, Jonas Lie, and Ibsen.

The greatest mistake of these writers—the one that has entirely escaped Max Nordau—is their belief that a nation can realize its best aspirations by methods that have utterly failed in the celestial empire of China. The hope of preserving the grand feature of the old Norwegian culture by exclusiveness, by isolating Norway, and by offering a stubborn resistance to foreign influence, be it good or bad—in this they have set themselves an impossible task. A thorough national life and development produced by such artificial means would, even if attended by the highest degree of success, partake of a theatrical nature. The more it succeeded, the more it would attract foreigners, and features which in olden times sprang from the character of the people and from natural circumstances, would fall into the line of carnivals organized at the expense of the municipalities and of railways to Alpine summits.

These Norwegian enthusiasts have yet to learn that, though foreign tourists, foreign literature, and foreign art place temptations in the way of their single-minded nation, there are in every country large numbers of people who fight for progress as sedulously as themselves, and whose co-operation would outweigh the dangers of European modernity.

In the old culture, in the past life of nations, especially in nations like Norway, there are great virtues and noble features which may well serve as a goal. But to again render them a reality, to base them on lasting foundations, a people must pass through the fiery trials of modern temptations, and, instead of yielding plastically to outward circumstances, must shape their destiny through sheer strength of character. What Norway has of good and noble she should give to other nations, and freely accept their best from them. This is an exchange which, like mercy, blesses both giver and receiver.

Though the struggle against degeneration is, in Norway, hampered by the national prejudices of the leaders, it is still progressing. Ibsen's mission in the fight is to ruthlessly expose the stagnant pools of corruption. He finds them in the cities and among the middle class, where the old German Philistine features have been most distinctly preserved. Many of his characters bear German names, and those who take the part of the traditional villain wear often the garb of that respectable, common-sense, matter-of-fact, self-absorbed German whom Max Nordau would exempt from any stigma of degeneration.

Thorvald Helmer, in "The Dolls' House," has, or would have, the sympathies of millions, not in

Germany alone, but in England and everywhere, of people whose emotional nature, whose love for the high and noble, has been compressed by that worldly wisdom which in our large crowded cities becomes prudence, and to obey which is often a duty—people who are not aware that it is not only possible, but even easy, to be both diplomatic and discreet in obedience to noble emotions and exalted aspirations, and that to root these out of our nature is degeneration.

Helmer, in his sleek reasonableness, is an excellent type of meanness, and his character is brought out in a consummately artistic way. It exasperates Max Nordau that this man, who comes so near his standard of sound-mindedness, should inspire in audiences all the world over, especially in the female element, a sense of aversion, apparently without any effort on the part of the author. Helmer has a keen eye for the main chance. His reputation and his position have his first consideration. He trembles at the idea of fighting the world without them. His love of his wife is the quintessence of selfishness. He loves her in the two only ways which Max Nordau thinks reasonable in a human being, as a companion, as a pleasant thing to toy with; and as the female of his race, at such periods when he, as the normal man of Max Nordau, is actuated by animal impulses, for example, under the influence of champagne. Of the pure love for a woman which in a man's heart remains as a spring of living water, giving him a pang of joy each time his thoughts revert to her, and which casts a rosy tint of poetry over life, nay even over death—of such love Helmer is as incapable as Max Nordau's normal man.

Nora yearns for the higher, nobler love, and her lack of experience in character-study has left her in doubt, though in hope, regarding her husband. The moment comes when she gains certitude ; and when Helmer reveals himself in his Philistine hideousness, her spirit revolts.

Though of course exaggerated for the sake of dramatic effect, she is a good type of an intelligent and emotional Norwegian woman. Norwegian girls receive a great deal of instruction, and as they have no professions to prepare for, their education is more literary and artistic than that of the men. They read voraciously the Norwegian modern writers, and sympathize consequently more than the men with the extreme nationalists. They are often strongly possessed by the *Aand*—that indefinable yearning for all that is great and noble—in Norwegian culture already alluded to. They have a fair knowledge of foreign literature, and read a great many English novels. With their admiration for English pure love, for English home life, grafted on the grand aspirations which the new *Aand* fosters, they may well appear uncanny and troll-like to the prosaic German.

We trust that the struggle between the Norwegian and the German cultures, of which we have endeavoured to give an idea, will make it easier for students of Ibsen to understand his characters. It is in "The Doll's House" where the two inimical cultures are most clearly personified, the old Norwegian culture being represented by the uncompromising, impulsive, and intense Nora, and the imported German culture by the pedantic, commonplace, and animal Helmer.

If our interpretation is right, it is impossible that Ibsen's work could in any way indicate degeneration. It ought, on the contrary, to be evident that his pieces, rendering objective as they do the struggle for a higher and better life, based not on pedantic considerations of immediate and unworthy advantages, but on the noble impulses of a strong and healthy nation, are at once a summons to rise higher, and signals pointing the way.

CHAPTER VIII

RICHARD WAGNER

WE all have met with people who, without being degenerates to any great extent, repeat stories of their own invention so persistently, that they end by believing in them. In this kind of folly, if folly it be, there is a great deal of method when indulged in by people who are anxious, for some reason or another, that their views should *nolens volens* be accepted by others. When one comes to deal with the intellectual development of a nation or a race, and wishes to prove certain forms of progress or retrogression, it is half the battle to bring your opponent to believe in the existence of some special, well-defined psychological phenomenon or social tendency, and to give it a high-sounding name. What would astrology have been without the horoscope, or alchemy without the philosopher's stone? What would modern statecraft be without such terms as "foreign competition" and "international jealousy"? What would German socialism be without the term "revoutionary socialism"? What would bi-metallism be without the phrase, "the stability of the currency"? And what would Max Nordau's theory of degeneration be without the "mystic movement"?

He takes for granted that there is such a thing as mysticism, as well as that it constitutes a movement, and then endeavours to explain everything as partaking of or resulting from it. According to him, Wagnerism is the reappearance in Germany of that romanticism which originated there, and afterwards travelled through France and England. It reappeared, according to him, through Wagner's degeneration, and spread in virtue of the degeneration of his contemporaries. He says that he finds in Wagner a greater abundance of degeneration than in all the other degenerates put together. "The stigmata of his morbid condition," he says, "are united in him in the most complete and most luxuriant development."

This is a bold assertion, and will appear bolder yet to any one who has read his chapter in "The Richard Wagner Cult." Wagner's dislike of the Jews, which Max Nordau calls anti-semitism, and his views on social questions, which our alienist calls Anarchism, are pointed out as unfailing stigmata of degeneration. One of the methods of our alienist is to notice and make much of certain extreme opinions in people who are actually made, or who have made themselves, intensely objectionable, and then to point out that similar opinions and ideas are present in the mind of some celebrity, and then to draw the conclusion that this celebrity must be on the road to madness. Either he does not see himself, or he trusts his readers will not see, that by such methods every man in the world might be proved to some extent deranged. He forgets that exaggerated virtues become vices, and that some of the most prominent men in the world have had idiosyncrasies to which they have even given considerable play without at all coming within the range of degeneration.

The anti-semitism in Germany, which Max Nordau ascribes to degeneration—probably with the approval of the majority of Jews—in that country, as well as in Russia, France, and the United States, springs from causes so patent, that no man who aspires to be considered an acute observer of his time should ignore them.

Let us instance Russia first—a country where the latest wave of anti-semitism first took a violent form. Can any one who is acquainted with the typical financial history of the Russian villages wonder that the Jews in Russia should be looked upon as a scourge? What has happened in thousands of such villages is this. An energetic, clever Jew settles amongst the Russian Moujiks, who combine thriftlessness and love of an easy life with many of the good qualities and innocence of primitive races. The Jew is bent on making money, and caring little about the opinion the community may form of him, and too brave to fear their enmity, he has no hesitation in taking up any kind of business, however unpopular it may render him. He willingly becomes a publican, a pawnbroker, a landgrabber, and, in combination with other Jews, a speculator and cornerer. His attention to business, his self-denial, his hardheartedness to his customers, his knowledge of the tricks of trades and finance, the ready support he gets from his co-religionists in other districts in carrying out his purposes, however derogatory they may be to the community—all this soon renders him the master of the situation. The stranger, who at first in such a friendly spirit invited his customer to drink his *vodka* and borrow his money, is soon transformed into a harsh tyrant who, by hook or by crook, came into possession of all the belongings of the villagers, and calmly makes use of their destitution to extort from them their future earnings. The Jews, as a rule, on the one hand, and the Russians on the other, form diametrically opposite views on this social phenomenon. The Jews say, and Max Nordau evidently sides with them, that this successful Jewish village tyrant has done nothing to deserve blame. He has only been more frugal, more thrifty and more intelligent than the Russians, who were bound by their inferior character to go to the wall; and that if Russia hates the Jews, it is with that hatred against successful men common in human failures.

The ruined Russian peasants simply know that the Jew who came among them is rich and they are poor, that what used to be their possessions form his wealth, and that the means he has used to obtain it would not have been used by them under any circumstances. They think they have been robbed, and that they and their descendants would be robbed by the Jew and his descendants if they cannot be freed from him. Hence anti-semitism in Russia.

Max Nordau has no right to call the anti-semitists degenerate, even though they be wrong in their logic because he is wrong himself, and he cannot point to ruined homes and wrecked lives as a substantial foundation for his opinion.

In Germany the Jews play the same part, though under modified conditions. Though bad, German laws and German officialism are better than those of Russia, and the German people do not so easily fall a prey to the strong-minded Jew. But, on the other hand, the Jews make themselves obnoxious in other ways, both in Germany and Austria. Here they act everywhere as trade-spoilers. The Jew undersells everybody. He stops short of nothing, save breaking the law, to extend his business. He is obsequious to those in power and in wealth, but relentlessly hard to competitors and to creditors. Many of them will take the greatest possible advantage of other people's, especially Christians', misfortunes, and will gain their end by deliberately wounding other people's feelings. It is the Jews who generally pay the lowest wages, and who are found in the ranks of the sweaters.

We hasten to state that there are in Germany a great many exceptions to the types here referred to. But either they are not numerous enough, or the Jew must possess some inability to show his better qualities, for no one acquainted with the circumstances in Germany would deny that the Jew-haters there look upon their enemies in exactly the light we have described.

But this is not all. Accusations are levelled against the Jews which are partly untrue, or else vastly exaggerated, and those who make them should be called upon to prove their statements. Whether they may be able to do this or not, the fact remains that the Jew-hating Germans believe that the Jews have formed one vast conspiracy, the object of which is to secure for the Jews large advantages at the expense of the Christians. It is alleged that the methods employed are as follows : the Jews are supposed to meet in secret conclave, in which those of them who desire to accomplish any special aim state it to their brethren, who then combine in assisting them. Such aims may be the possession of a house or a shop in the hands of a Christian, the ruin of some obnoxious competitor, the miscarriage of some public auction of goods coveted by some Jew, and so on. With such ideas prevailing, how is it possible to ascribe Jew hatred to degeneracy? Such logic is all the more surprising as it remains a palpable fact that the fortunes of the Jewish houses are growing apace, that Jews seem to succeed no matter what they undertake, that they certainly are more charitable to their co-religionists than to Christians, and for that matter than Christians are to Christians, while at the same time poverty and misery are on the increase among the Christian masses.

Max Nordau does a bad service to the Jews of Germany when he attempts to lay the blame for anti-semitism exclusively at the door of the Christians and calls them degenerates, while he entirely exempts the Jews. This partiality, coupled with his contempt for the masses and his belief in government by the more strong-minded men, points to a future state in Germany in which the Jews should be the ruling aristocracy. His unfairness thus, instead of abating the persecution against the Jews, might easily be construed into an excuse for a more bitter anti-semitism.

This error of his is due to his besetting habit of taking his postulates from doubtful authorities and of drawing illogical conclusions. It is a common thing for men who have been successful in one branch of knowledge, and who are regarded as authorities in a specialty by others, to jump at rash conclusions with regard to subjects on which authorities differ or do not exist. This is exactly what Max Nordau does when he comes to consider facts which cannot be rightly understood without a clear insight into sociology and other social sciences. He then evinces impossible opinions, and gives us to understand that he has a ready-made scheme for reconstructing society on a new and perfect plan.

It is not difficult to see what this plan is. It is quasi-Collectivism and Communism. He wishes the State to become the universal heir of all fortunes and the universal benefactor. The absurdity and impracticability of this scheme—which, by the way, is always the very one that first enters the head of a young student who tackles social science for the first time—are obvious. As however he does not insist upon his scheme in his volume "Degeneration," it would be out of place to explain its hollowness here. We have referred to it simply to show that his superficiality regarding the anti-semitic question is not incidental. It will be evident to anybody who tackles this question with an unprejudiced mind that the

Christians in Russia and Germany are utterly at fault when they believe that they can escape from their troubles by persecuting Jews, and also that the Jews are utterly at fault when they attribute anti-semitism to the jealousy and wickedness of the Christians. Both these parties, as well as Max Nordau himself, allow their feelings instead of their intelligence to determine these questions. But they are not necessarily degenerate.

The true explanation of the imbroglio is as follows : The Jewish race, which might have acquired a few unpleasant characteristics by no fault of their own but through a cruel and unjust persecution for centuries, is a highly-gifted one, distinguishing itself by strong-mindedness, great will-power, remarkable powers of endurance, morality, and singleness of purpose. Deprived, in a great number of countries of social rights and the privileges of citizenship, they have for centuries found only one way open to them by which they could attain to independence, security, and consideration—the accumulation of wealth. In modern times, when social institutions and laws tend to render wealth almost omnipotent, its acquisition has become to this people of greater importance than ever. Success in a business, however small, may mean millions in the future, while failure may result in life-long misery. Consequently, the Jews apply themselves to their trades or professions with an energy and assiduity such as few races can command.

They therefore represent a power in the development of humanity which is bound to produce far-reaching effects. Whether these will constitute a blessing or a curse to the nations among whom the Jews live and work depends entirely on the institutions and the laws of those countries. If these are such as to render the oppression of the poor, the workers, the borrowers, the tenants—in fact, all the sections of society on which the Jews now batten—a condition for the thriving of the capitalists, the employers, the lenders, the tenants, and the fortunate classes in general—if the laws are of this description, then the Jews will be conspicuous as the oppressors of others. But if, on the contrary, the laws and institutions of the countries are such as to render the success of the upper classes and leaders of trade, industry, and finance dependent on the welfare of the workers, then the Jews will be the most liberal lenders, the most generous employers, and the most accommodating landlords. In fact, the question resolves itself simply into one of demand and supply; as long as there is a greater demand for Jews' services than the Jews are able to supply, the latter will dominate; but when there are more services offered on the part of the Jews than the people can avail themselves of, these can dictate terms to the Jews. And this relation of demand and supply depends on laws and institutions.

Even if Max Nordau's prejudices prevented him from taking this view of the anti-semitic question—which is not only the correct one but which greatly facilitates the solution of the question, and thus would prevent the disgraceful persecution which in many countries threatens to become more serious—he might have found, by simply looking at the actualities, in the different countries that anti-semitism prevails in an inverse ratio to good government. He could not have asked for a better proof of the fact that laws and institutions are at fault and not the Jews or the Christians. To take only the two extremes: in Russia, where the government, from the people's point of view, is probably the worst in Europe, anti-semitism is most vehement; in England, where the government is more influenced by the consideration of the good of the people than any other country, there is scarcely any animosity against the Jews, and this in spite of the efforts of certain politicians to promote it.

The reception of Dr. Stöcker, when he attempted to address a public meeting in London in favour of anti-semitism, would have convinced Max Nordau, had he been present, what a poor chance anti-semitism has in a country where the working classes are free to follow those instincts which Max

Nordau fears so much. We may relate that hardly had the proceedings begun when the hall was filled by labourers, who, contrary to their habit on such occasions, had not changed their dress, and who hooted Dr. Stöcker, stormed the platform, overpowered the anti-semitists, and cleared the hall.

In face of the fact that anti-semitic questions turn so entirely on prejudices and mistakes, one cannot surely accuse Wagner of madness because he sided with what may be called a national party, and approved of a movement the object of which was to stay the progressive influence of an alien race over the destiny of the Fatherland.

In several places in his work Max Nordau insists upon considering the anarchist tendencies of our age as among the stigmata of degeneration. If he were right, we should be face to face with a calamity likely to end in the brutalization or the annihilation of our race. For Anarchism in some form or another is certainly spreading rapidly. That there is Anarchism and Anarchism seems of little importance to our alienist in his eagerness to draw his pre-conceived conclusions. He reasons as usual. Starting from the hypothesis that some of the criminal Anarchists were, to some extent, mentally deranged and morally weak, he arrives at the conclusion that Wagner was a degenerate, because he shared to some extent with the Anarchists the hatred of our present social system and of the injurious effects it produces on the masses of the people.

Though Max Nordau dwells far more lengthily on poetry, and art, and cognate subjects than on the graver question of Anarchism, there is no point on which it behoves us better to set him and his readers right than that of the relation between Anarchism and degeneration.

The Anarchist is not a cause. He is an effect. There is a feeling in the consciousness of almost every human being, be he a believer in a divine religion or in Max Nordau's religion of humanity, that our race is destined to a high degree of development, and to a far larger sphere of happiness than now falls to the lot of most of us. This yearning for happiness, for elevation, is not only a feeling but a conviction consequent upon our knowledge of the past stages of the development of man.

There was a time when fervent religious beliefs induced patience and resignation under suffering, and when our future destiny was left in the hands of Providence. But the French encyclopædists, and after them the modern scientists, have done their best to undermine this belief and to show us that the destiny of future generations will largely depend upon us and themselves, that science is placing in our hands an ever-growing control over the forces of nature, and that if humanity suffers it is because the present generation has not the moral courage to throw off religious scruples and boldly shape their own destiny.

These doctrines, in unison with the general progressive spirit of the age, led to revolutions and political reforms. In the absence of a Providence the nations shifted their faith to constitutional governments. But the new faith did not last long. The more democratic the governments were the more they applied the principles of Collectivism—they yielded to those instincts which Max Nordau calls the social instincts. Under the pretext of exercising paternal kindness towards the people, the governments demanded paternal rights. Communistic and socialistic ideas spread among the masses, who, well aware that a Providence without power would be no providence at all, wanted to render the State omnipotent. When however socialistic features were introduced into the constitutions, matters did not mend, but the freedom of the individual was more and more infringed.

When detailed schemes of further socialistic development were made public, a great many freedom-loving men and women beheld with terror that the chief cause of the favour with which the progressing socialism was regarded was to be found in the plan of complete subjection of the individual under government.

This discovery naturally caused a reaction in favour of liberty. Those who became Anarchists felt keenly the claws of the State upon them, and they foresaw that more socialism would aggravate their grievances. They took for granted that humanity had now tried all forms of government and that they had all failed, and that the salvation of the race could only be found in absolute personal freedom.

The first extreme Russian Nihilists paved the way for the Anarchist movement in Europe. They, like their first followers in France, had only one idea, that of destroying at all costs the present order of things, and thus clearing the ground for a new system to grow up free from the tyranny of governments, aristocracies, militarism, landlordism, and capitalism.

They saw that an immense mass of poor, hardworking, honest people with but a small chance of happiness for themselves, but imbued with a strong desire to see the whole of humanity happy, were oppressed by a small number of selfish people who arrogated to themselves the lion's share of the good things of life. They found that this band of selfish people attained to their immense power by a social system of slow and gradual growth.

Tracing all the troubles to the few egotists whom they regarded as criminals, they imagined that by destroying them and the system, the unselfish and humanitarian aspirations of the masses would blossom forth free and unvitiated.

The Anarchists were thus the backbone of the religion of humanity, only their faith was stronger than that of Max Nordau, for they were willing to sacrifice all, including life, for the good of the race.

If these people were, and are, degenerate, then every mistake in reasoning is a sign of degeneration, and faith in humanity and its destiny is the beginning of madness.

When Max Nordau designates Wagner as an Anarchist, he evidently ignores the fact that there are two kinds of Anarchists, the violent ones just described, and the moderate or constitutional ones. The latter call themselves simply Anarchists. Their numbers are growing rapidly in France, as well as in England, and in both these countries Max Nordau would be surprised at their moderation and common sense. The movement they represent is a reaction against the socialistic tendencies, and their programme is not violence and destruction, but the gradual abolition of all harmful and useless legislation. It is true that so far they have no precise policy. But such special measures as are advocated — partly in France, partly in

England, and partly in the United States—seem to be founded on clear and thorough reasoning, and when their leading principle is compared with the shallow chatter of socialists and communists of every school it appears as wisdom itself.

What all these people believe, what they long for, and what they hope for, is exactly what Wagner believed, longed for, and hoped for. He saw in Philistinism, in official tyranny, in police government, and in legal trammels standing in the way of trades, industries, and arts, so many impediments to the realization of the best instincts and the highest aspirations of humanity. Whatever opinions he held, they can only be judged by the few exasperated exclamations he gave vent to with regard to the corruption of modern society. It is not likely that he, with such immense works on hand, should have given sufficient attention to social questions to allow him to express himself in learned terms. But what he said and wrote on the subject shows clearly that the foundation of his social views was trust in humanity, in the sanctity of nature, and in the ennobling power of liberty. Can any one with a true love of art imagine an artist without such a creed?

What was more natural than that, fêted and praised as he was, he should have a good opinion of his own talent and consider himself a great man. If for this he deserved to be suspected of megalomania, what are we to say about other celebrities, mediocrities, and nonenties, who imagine themselves demigods because they happen to be the sons of their fathers, to be born in purple, or to have a title attached to their name?

Max Nordau is extremely hard on those who have sung the praises of Wagner, and insinuates that they have been actuated by base motives when they have not been absolutely degenerated. According to him, admiration for Wagner's works is a sure sign of mental unsoundness. And yet this same Max Nordau finds reasons for praising Wagner's genius which a host of his panegyrists have overlooked. He says: " Wagner, as a dramatist is really a historical painter of the highest rank. . . . This (a fresco painter) he is in a degree never yet attained by any other dramatic author in the whole world of literature. Every action embodies itself for him in a series of most imposing pictures, which, when they are composed as Wagner has seen them with his inner eye, must overwhelm and enrapture the beholder. The reception of the guests in the hall of Wartburg; the arrival and departure of Lohengrin in the boat drawn by the swan; the gambols of the Rhine maidens in the river; the defiling of the gods over the rainbow-bridge towards the castle of Asgard; the bursting of the moonlight into Hunding's hut; the ride of the Walküre over the battle-field; Brunhilde in the circle of fire; the final scene in "Götterdämmerung," where Brunhilde flings herself on to her horse and leaps into the midst of the funeral pyre, while Hagan throws himself into the surging Rhine, and the heavens are aflame with the glow from the burning palace of the gods; the lovefeast of the knights in the castle of the Grail; the obsequies of Titurel and the healing of Amfortas — these are pictures to which nothing in art hitherto approaches."

It is strange that Max Nordau in his love for authorities should quote Nietzsche — a German author whom, in another part of his book, he makes out to be a hopeless degenerate and charlatan—in support of his views of Wagner! But Nietzsche has written a book called "Der Fall Wagner," and that suffices. This Nietzsche calls Wagner a comedian, but Nordau insists upon his being a painter, and that "if he had been a healthy genius, endowed with intellectual equilibrium, that is what he would undoubtedly have become. His inner vision would have forced the brush into his hand, and would have constrained him to use it on canvas by means of colour."

When Max Mordau says a painter, he evidently restricts the meaning of the word to its narrowest sense, and makes it difficult to at all class a man who, like Wagner, evolved and produced pictures of such grandeur and such beauty as those our alienist so well describes. The fact that the artist uses actual perspective, real draperies, living people, actual fire, that he selects his own light, and personally arranges this mass of objects so as to exactly reproduce the daring conception of his mind — all this should surely not be cited as so many proofs of the unhealthiness of his genius. Would he have been a greater, a sounder genius, had his ability been restricted to sketching and colouring his conceptions on cardboard or canvas? Should then a painter's genius be confined to the production of pictures suitable only to decorate Philistine houses and official galleries? Because Max Nordau's pedantic tendencies have formed such a Philistine idea about the art of painting, is it right to deny true genius to a man who has produced unapproachable pictures on a colossal scale, not by the means of brushes and pigments, but by materials infinitely more difficult to handle.

But these masterpieces of painting do not alone bear witness to Wagner's powers. His paintings are not fixed; they are movable. They represent actually an enchanting succession of pictures. The true genius *à la* Nordau gives us the pictures of figures in motion that never move, and tires us with a Quintus Curtius suspended in mid-air half way down a chasm, until we wish him at the bottom of it. Such a moving picture of Wagner's is not thrust upon us suddenly in the manner of gallery pictures, but is presented to us as the fit illustration of a beautiful poem, and often as the climax of a series of other pictures which explain it, relieve it and work up our emotions for its reception.

To this must be added that the same painter-genius, the same dramatist, the same poet, has created the wondrous and enchanting music which accompanies the poem and the pictures. And because he has done all this, because he has not followed the routine of other German painters, because he has dared to, and succeeded in, transporting his audiences into the highest possible region of imagination, and given them a glimpse of real creative powers, he is to be classed as a degenerate; to rank among those of whom humanity is ashamed, and whose degraded state is to warn us of the coming decay of our race.

Can any one with a grain of humour read Max Nordau's attacks on Wagner without imagining an irascible toy-terrier barking at the moon?

Max Nordau probably feels that Wagner's anti-semitism, his Anarchism, and his ability to create transcendentally beautiful pictures, are stigmata which hardly any of his readers would accept as such, and consequently feels impelled to make much of what it pleases him to call Wagner's eroticism. Here, as everywhere in his book, in order to impress his readers he counts on the mystical effect which the use of a high-sounding scientific word generally produces upon unscientific readers. A favourite expression of his, when speaking of some psychological phenomenon, is that science knows all about it, and he calls it megalomania, graphomania, echolalia, or some such name. With people who have only a superficial knowledge of science, and who stand in awe of its achievements, such nouns stand for a special definite thing, thoroughly investigated and explained. They do not know that these scientific names have been invented, not in order to designate something real and palpable, but simply for the purpose of bringing order into an arbitrary classification, invented so that the exchange of ideas may be facilitated on the subject thus treated. Such scientific terms might even be classed among mystical symbols, in so far as they often stand for something of which hardly anything is known, but at the same time serve the same useful end as algebraical figures. Psychologists are prone to speak of a man's consciousness, though scarcely two scientific men would agree as to what it is. But this does not prevent them from dividing consciousness up into divisions and sub-divisions, all with their special names, in order to be able to express their ideas in words. The unscientific reader should bear in mind that consciousness has never been under the microscope, or in the crucible, and that the classification of the scientists has no counterpart in consciousness itself, and that this remains the impalpable and indivisible *Ego*, with its infinite number of attributes inseparably commingled. All the different states, conditions, faculties, perfections and defects of the *Ego* are of course known only by the results they produce in the physical world, and it is by these results that they have been classified. It is evident that such methods of classification should leave an immense margin for those who wish, or feel impelled by their own idiosyncrasies, to misuse scientific terms designating psychological phenomena.

Max Nordau indulges in this misuse of scientific terms to the fullest extent, in a way not to be easily discovered by the non-scientific reader. The word "eroticism" used by him so frequently, with all the pomposity of a scientific term, is coined from the word "erotic," a literary term which again is derived, as we all know, from Eros, the Greek god of love. It is an adjective which means pertaining to or expressive of love-passion. Such an adjective necessarily finds an enormously wide application, considering that love in one sense is the leading principle in organic creation, and, in a more psychological sense, the motive power in the human drama. We may say that we ourselves, the outcome of love, regulate our whole life, and sometimes base our hopes of a future state on love. Consequently there is hardly anything in our lives that is not covered by the adjective "erotic."

The alienists having adopted the word "eroticism" in order to designate a state of mind which certain actions reveal to them, and which state of mind, when its existence is corroborated by other facts, may be considered as a disease, it is evident that, while they may apply the word eroticism to almost anything in the organic world and in human society, it is better for their purpose to apply it only to a certain form of a diseased mind. While a strictly logical and careful alienist might deem it irrational and confusing to use the term "eroticism," or even the adjective "erotic," outside a clearly defined case of mental disease, it cannot be considered absolutely wrong to apply such terms whenever the love-passion is in question, even a love-passion of a most legitimate kind.

We shall now show how Max Nordau manages to slip over the border within which scientific terms should be used, and applies them indiscriminately to everything; and how he, in this manner, tries to establish that Wagner suffers from erotic madness, because he looks upon love as one of the chief motors in the human drama and the tree of knowledge for good or evil.

Max Nordau, in a flippant criticism, which he endeavours to render funny, of the behaviour of Wagner's characters on the stage, forgets his self-criticism to such an extent as to liken them to mad tom-cats—a simile which probably no sane man would accept as true. Having once conceived the idea of mad tom-cats, it at once becomes an obsession in his mind, and suggests presentations of real cases of erotic fury. He consequently, according to his habit, takes for granted that the actors on the stage must necessarily represent the exact state of mind of the author, and cries out that this state of the author's mind (which he has persuaded himself is that of a mad tom-cat) is well known to science, and is called Sadism. Then, with a regret at having to touch upon such subjects in order to make his readers understand Wagner's real mental condition, he gives a disgusting example of a maniac whose erotic madness has brought him below the level of the brute.

This is a fair sample of Max Nordau's logic. For the sake of clearness, we recapitulate the logical *tour de force* he has been compelled to exercise in order to arrive at such an absurdity : Wagner, like all poets and dramatists before him, creates a love scene. Love is an erotic emotion. Eroticism is a disease of the mind. Tom-cats are erotically influenced. The characters on the stage remind Max Nordau of tom-cats. The obsession of a "tom-cat in convulsions over a root of valerian" suggests a raving madman. Consequently Wagner is mad.

Such is the use a scientist is tempted to make of his science when he throws self-criticism overboard.

When Max Nordau says of Wagner that he has been all his life an erotic, he is fair enough to add in parenthesis, "in a psychiatric sense." But this is not enough. The word "psychiatric" is a strictly scientific word, not to be found in any ordinary English dictionary; and the ordinary reader might easily conclude that, instead of removing Wagner's eroticism into the deep recesses of his soul, it might have been used by the author, as so many scientific words have been used, in order to aggravate his charge.

In order to justify his opinion with regard to Wagner's erotic madness, he says: "The most ordinary incitements, even those farthest removed from the province of sexual instincts, never fail to awaken in his consciousness voluptuous images of an erotic character." Why "sexual instincts"? Why not love-instincts, an expression which had so much better fitted in with the scenes Wagner represents? But, as it suits Max Nordau's purpose to keep his reader's mind upon love in its lowest, most animal form, we shall let it pass. We must however express our astonishment at the example he gives in order to show how incitements, " far removed from the province of sexual instincts," caused Wagner's mind to revert to voluptuous images. The "farthest removed incitements" which Max Nordau quotes is the description by Wagner of a ballet—a *pas de trois*—evidently intended to represent the blending of the beautiful with love, to give Wagner's own words, " Love and life, the joy and wooing of art." What on earth, then, would more arouse such eroticism that might be found in a man than a ballet representing love and life? And this especially when we consider the modern freedom with regard to the costume of ballet girls. In order to show what Max Nordau considers to be the outcome of erotic madness in Wagner's choregraphic representation of love, life, and art, we give *in extenso* the passage from " Art-Work of the Future," to which he refers:

" In the contemplation of this ravishing dance of the most genuine and noblest muses of the artistic man, we now see the three arm in arm lovingly entwined up to their necks; then this, then that one, detaching herself from the entwinement, as if to display to the others her beautiful form in complete separation, touching the hands of the others only with the extreme tips of her fingers; now the one, entwined by a backward glance at the twin forms of her closely entwined sisters, bending towards them; then two, carried away by the allurements of the one greeting her in homage; finally all, in close embrace, breast to breast, limb to limb, in an ardent kiss of love, coalescing in one blissfully living shape. This is the love and life, the joy and wooing of art," etc.

When Max Nordau wishes to traduce the love scenes in Wagner's operas into arguments of the musician's erotic madness, he forgets many things. He forgets what he himself has given as a test of a sound mind, namely, the ability to look after one's own business. Even if Wagner had produced scenes on his stage of an utterly corrupt character in order to gain money and popularity, he having succeeded completely in such objects, could not possibly be called mad by a critic who has made material success in life a test for soundmindedness, and who declares the belief in personal responsibility reaching beyond the grave to be a sign of madness. But he also forgets, what is more important, that there is no line of demarcation drawn to indicate how far the representation of human passions may be carried on the stage.

Even Max Nordau does not seem to have discovered an authority on this subject. He himself will not serve as an authority, because he has shown himself too apt to fall into the error of newspaper critics, that of judging a work or a piece, not according to its merits, but according to the author who has produced it. He would praise in Goethe what he would condemn in Wagner. If we were to indiscriminately ask people how far we may go in representing human passion on the stage, we should get a mass of replies all differing according to the bias of the respondents. The Ultramontane abbé, the zealous Methodist, would differ enormously from the Bohemian artist; the prudish old maid would differ from the poet. Nay, even two artists, both painters of the nude, or two ballet girls appearing in the same costume, might hold almost opposite opinions on this subject. How then shall we judge? By leaving out of court all the extremists—those who object to theatres, ballets, and nature in art—as well as those who would clamour for indecent and obscene representations, we might considerably narrow the ground for inquiry, and elicit certain rules likely to meet the suffrages of the majority within these limits. It might be argued that emotions, playing by far the most important *rôle* in the human drama, and lying as they do at the root of all our actions, educational agencies and amusements ought to be appealed to by the arts. Also that art in affording us opportunities of giving expression to our emotions, elevates and ennobles our lives: consequently, that the passive objective contemplation of human emotions which the stage affords us, helps us to study our own emotions and to bring them into harmony with our noblest aspirations, our future happiness, our judgment, and our will. In order to accomplish their mission, such representations should be as true to life as possible, whether they be beautiful or not. On this plea, it would be legitimate to represent on the stage erotic emotions in the full strength in which we meet with them in reality among sound-minded people. A good deal of exaggeration may be permitted to the actor as he is under the difficulty of having to convey by actions, gestures or facial expression a distinct representation of emotions which may rage in the consciousness of a human being without betraying themselves in physical signs.

From this it must be concluded that the purity of the stage depends more on what is acted than how it is acted. The author who does not wish to desecrate the drama is therefore bound to represent emotions which are the outcome of natural life, and acted upon by incidents such as we see around us, and to avoid the representation of, even if he cannot avoid the reference to, emotions which spring from a diseased mind or a morbid moral state.

Love, being an emotion to which every sound-minded being may be subject, there would be no objection to represent it in the most intense manner on the stage so long as we understand under the name of love that strong degree of affection which sometimes people of the opposite sex may conceive for each other apart from sexual emotions. What makes Max Nordau's reasoning plausible is that he does not admit that this kind of love exists. He distinguishes only two degrees, or two categories, of love, comradeship or friendship, on the one hand, and the animal instinct on the other. But no one who has gone through life with open eyes can possibly deny the reality of what we here, for want of a better expression, would call pure love. Everywhere we meet with manifestations of it. Even young children, who might have no idea of sexual emotion, often love each other with a genuine passion which sometimes lasts through life. Adults may be so absorbed in love for each other as to prefer death to separation, and yet never experience any sexual emotion in each other's company. Men and women lovers who have been separated have wasted away from sheer love of each other, and yet been remarkably chaste in character. In the English-speaking countries, where the relations between the sexes are free and natural, we find any number of proofs of the reality of pure love. Those cases alone which have ended tragically, and therefore come before the public, more than suffice to prove it. Even in countries like France, for example, where the sexual instincts are apt to become morbid from the one-sided education of the young, it is not difficult to find examples of pure love. It is even to be found where least expected, as, for instance, between a licentious man and a fallen woman. It is true that when pure love runs its usual course it gets, so to say, inflamed by animal passion, but this is generally the case only as a result of the demonstrations by which pure love tries to manifest itself. It may also be true that there exists a mysterious, that is to say, a so far unexplained connection between the purest love and sexual instinct even in loving couples to whom sexuality may be an abomination. But all this does not disprove that, speaking from a practical and ethical point of view, there is such an emotion as pure love, and that this emotion is a powerful motor in the human drama.

If it then be a fact that this yearning to love and to be loved with a pure love exists, and ought to exist, in rational human beings, and that in running its natural course it will manifest itself in demonstrations extremely likely to rouse animal passions, the question arises how far a love scene on the stage may display those demonstrations which, while they are the only possible means of expressing pure love, at the same time suggest sexual emotions.

Here then is the point where the difference

will arise, and where we may well be careful whose decision we accept. Can we do better than Wagner did—leave the audience to decide?

Wagner's German audiences, described by Max Nordau as including wives and daughters, have, to his great bewilderment, given the verdict in favour of Wagner's most passionate scenes. "How unperverted," Max Nordau cries out, "must wives and maidens be, when they are in a state of mind to witness these pieces without blushing crimson, and sinking to the earth for shame!" No. They have not blushed in following calmly and serenely the objective representations of passions which by nature have been implanted in every breast. The very vehemence, the very naturalness of the scenes inspire that awe and reverence which great natural forces always do, and the young girl in the audience does not for a moment revert to any impure representations or animal promptings which might have come within her experience, because she is æsthetically and not sexually excited. But if Max Nordau could watch her when she reads the above quoted passage in his book, he would see her blush deeply, not at the memory of Wagner's scenes, but at the feeling of having the first seed of degeneration sown in her heart.

Among the phrases used by Max Nordau in order to inculcate his readers with the idea that

Wagner, instead of being the very essence of an artist, one of the greatest practically creative geniuses of the world, is a mere erotic maniac, is this one—" all his ideas revolve about woman." While this phrase may lead the unwary reader astray, it throws a vivid light on the extent to which Max Nordau's opinion with regard to the relation of the sexes has been influenced by his continental bias. This ought to be made clear to his readers. Such expressions, if of any use at all in Max Nordau's reasoning, presuppose that it is quite an unusual thing for the ideas of poets, dramatists, and writers of fiction to revolve about woman. For our alienist does not refer to Wagner's private life. He is speaking only of Wagner, the author. The actual fact, of course, is that love and women have from times immemorial been the subject of legends, fairy tales, troubadour songs, poems, romances, novels, and dramas. Thus, according to the gospel of our alienist, all the past and present poetical authors of the world must have been, and are " subject to erotic madness," like Wagner.

There are, of course, men who, like Faust, devote their lives to intellectual pursuits and expend all their energy in forcing nature to yield up her secrets. But such men are not only exceptions—they may be looked upon as degenerates. This is what Faust at last discovered. He recognised that life was essentially emotional, and that by having crushed out his emotional nature he had failed to live his life. Whether Goethe intended to impart the lesson his "Faust" teaches us may be doubtful, but we can thus read it: we may suppress our emotional nature for a long time, but it will one day claim its rights, and, in its explosive escape from unnatural bondage, avenge itself on the suppressor, and hurl him to perdition. The emotions, Faust regrets, are all those inspired by women.

But the great majority of men do not suppress the emotions inspired by women, but, on the contrary, allow their whole lives to be influenced by them. To find confirmation of this fact in countries like France and Germany might not be so easy as in the English-speaking countries. Wherever the sexes are separated in youth, and where conventional marriages are the rule, the erotic impulses become over stimulated and lead to the excitement of animal passion. The love of the beautiful, all the æsthetic aspirations, the yearning for the society of women, the love of excitement, the chivalrous leanings, and the craving for pure love —all these are thrown as so much fuel into the furnace of sexual love. It is then that the struggle arises between the terrible demoniac love and pure love,—a struggle so frequently depicted in

Wagner's operas and which determines the lives of so many men on the Continent.

Part of the struggle of the continental man is to avoid the influence of women altogether, or else to look upon them after the manner of the Mahommedans. In countries therefore where pure love is left but little or no scope, the influence of women is not very marked, and certainly not acknowledged, because for a man to acknowledge it would be to avow himself an " erotic madman."

To understand the immense influence which a woman exercises over man's destiny and how closely men's minds "revolve about women," we must study the English-speaking countries where pure love has, if not free scope, freer scope than anywhere else, and where few healthy-minded men are ashamed to avow the value they place upon woman, her love, and her influence.

Despite the fact that Englishmen do not display towards women of all classes that engaging politeness, which favourably distinguishes Frenchmen, a stranger who visits England cannot fail soon to perceive in what high estimation woman is held. Her name is seldom taken in vain. There is no trace of that gross satire upon women which so often disfigures continental prints; she may be represented as sharp, worldly, extravagant, but rarely as immoral, unfaithful, or ugly. Some of the lower-class papers are strongly influenced by French views, but they never indulge in adaptations without some modification, and such papers as have been started in order to emulate the fast journals of Paris have always been extremely short-lived.

The same respect for women is manifest in fiction as well as on the stage. Here again in consequence of French influence we meet with women who have sinned, and women with a past, but they never play such degraded parts as they often do in French novels and plays. Ladies are allowed an extensive liberty, and they are rarely insulted; and obtain, even under trying circumstances, a respectful treatment at the hands of the lowest class of labourers. We have unfortunately amongst us ruffians who beat their wives, but in ninety-nine cases out of a hundred these are drunken and debauched human failures. The average working man treats his wife and his daughter with as much consideration as a nobleman could his, and their home is kept morally pure and as comfortable for the women as his resources allow. He is not ashamed to carry parcels, burdens, the children, or to perambulate the baby in public places in order to spare his wife the trouble.

The men most reluctantly suspect a woman of immorality, and generally not until there seems a strong case against her. Indecent words and allusions are entirely excluded in the presence of ladies, and if a woman in her innocence inadvertently makes a risky remark, it passes unheeded and without producing a smile.

The average Englishman's life brings him into constant contact with women, and he is perfectly aware that he owes to them much that is bright and happy in his existence. Already as a child he is the trusted protector of his sisters, and often the cavalier of their friends. Early in life he loves some young woman, and his long courtship is to him a happy time. When he works hard, when he risks his life on the sea or in dangerous climes, it is generally with a view to marrying the girl he loves. When he is married, he wishes to succeed that he may gain his wife's approval, beautify her home, and make her life happy; while at the same time he never remains insensible to the admiration of other women. While his wife is yet young, his daughters grow up and become important features in his life and his happiness.

It may therefore be said of the men of the English-speaking countries that their "ideas revolve about women," and it will be difficult to persuade us Englishmen that respect, admiration, and love for women are the signs of a degenerate mind. Coleridge well expresses the English feeling—a feeling which, under circumstances similar to those prevailing in England, would be universal :—

> "All thoughts, all passions, all delights,
> Whatever stirs this mortal frame,
> All are but ministers of Love,
> And feed his sacred flame."

Wagner's music, which may be said to have been the delight of millions of people, is not approved of by Max Nordau. He condemns it on the usual ground that it is novel, and that it differs from the standards accepted before Wagner. According to him, it is the music of an unsound mind, because it contains no distinct ideas in the shape of melodies. He objects to the *Leit-motiv* and to the unending melody, but it is difficult to harmonize what he says against the one with what he says against the other. Speaking of the *Leit-motiv*, he says : "To express ideas is not the function of music. Language provides for that as completely as could be desired. When the word is accompanied by song or orchestra, it is not to make it more definite, but to reinforce it by the intervention of emotion. Music is a kind of sounding-board in which the word has to awake something like an echo from the infinite." Later on he says about melody : "It is a regular grouping of notes in a highly expressive series of tones. Melody in music corresponds to what in language is a logically constructed sentence distinctly presenting an idea, and having a clearly marked beginning and ending."

Music being an art which exclusively appeals to emotion, it is not surprising that any attempt to measure its value by a reasoning process should result in utter failure. But this is no excuse for an author to contradict himself so flatly as Max Nordau does in the above passages. To say on one page that "*to express ideas is not the function of music,*" and on another page to say that "melody is indispensable to music, because it corresponds to a logically constructed sentence *distinctly presenting an idea.*" Again he says: "Melody may be said to be an effort to say something definite," and how can this harmonize with the other mission of music: "to awake something like an echo from the infinite." The latter expression is not only a true definition of the mission of music, but also an exact description of the aim of Wagner's music.

Max Nordau feels that his scientific reasoning about music will affect no one who has heard the music of Wagner, and that those who admire it will be slow to believe that an unsound mind could have accomplished such complicated, intricate, and complete work. To prepare his reader's mind for his rash conclusion, he once more goes to the lunatic asylum for his arguments, in order to show that a man may be a lunatic and yet be a good musician.

But here again he is strangely blind to the fact that such arguments tell directly against his theory. He cites cases of lunatics who "improvised on the piano," who "sang very beautiful airs and at the same time improvised two different themes on the piano . . . who composed very beautiful, new, and melodious tunes."

The remarkable thing about the music of his maniacs is that it is tuny and melodious, and consequently the only rational music, according to Max Nordau, while Wagner's music is condemned by him, and Wagner himself is held up as a lunatic because his music is not like that of acknowledged lunatics! It stands to reason that a weak mind could follow and repeat a style of music which it has heard for years, but that it requires a strong and sound mind to break a new road in the domain of music with the full approval of millions of musical people.

Max Nordau also feels the necessity of backing up his opinion by authorities. He sees a conclusive proof of Wagner's inferiority in the criticism of professional musicians and composers. He might as well form his opinion of an actress on the criticism of her by her most dangerous rival. It seems that Hiller and Schumann would not acknowledge Wagner's musical endowment, but attributed his success to the libretti written by himself. Regarding this Max Nordau exclaims: "The same old story: musicans regard him as a poet, and poets as a musician." This means that our alienist is, or pretends to be, so utterly innocent of humour and satire as to accept this very common way of minimizing the talent of a rival as a trustworthy judgment. It is the commonest thing in the world for a man to deny his rival's talent in his own speciality, and then, in order to strengthen the effect of his opinion and to give it the colour of impartiality, to acknowledge in him talents outside that speciality. Practical men, when they hear one musician run down another musician, generally conclude that the latter has a dangerous talent. Voltaire, in speaking of a writer none of whose works were in existence, said that he must have been a man of genius judging from the savage attacks made upon him by another writer.

Hiller and Schumann are the only authorities whom Max Nordau can point to in support of his views, and he himself raises some doubts whether their dislike of Wagner's music was not due to the difficulty of immediately appreciating a tendency so novel as Wagner's. Our alienist is only able to add that Rubinstein can only make some important reservations, and that it was some time before Hanslick struck his colours. In view, then, of the enormous literature that has grown up around Wagner and

Wagnerism, Max Nordau's habit of referring to authorities in this instance simply has the effect of showing that he stands unsupported in his opinion by all musical authorities. It is irresistibly comic to notice how Max Nordau regrets that the brochure in which Nietzche—in "Der Fall Wagner"—attacks Wagner is quite as "insanely delirious" as another brochure written by the same writer twelve years before in deification of Wagner. Had it not been for this awkward circumstance, Max Nordau, it seems, would have been only too glad to exalt Nietzsche—the man whom in another part of his work he strenuously endeavours to prove an imbecile—to the rank of an authority. His amazing lack of logic prevents him from seeing that a certificate of lunacy issued by a lunatic is really a certificate of sanity, in virtue of the logical axiom that two negatives are equal to one affirmative.

Such faults and defects as may be found in Wagner's prose writings have little importance in relation—and are almost irrevelant—to the question of his supposed degeneracy. He had to deal with subjects which, though intensely real to our emotional nature, can only be treated inadequately in words. Whatever we may think of Wagner's style, there can be little doubt that he has succeeded in making himself understood by a great number of people whose emotional nature sympathizes with that of

Wagner, and whom even Max Nordau would not undertake to prove to be mentally deranged or morally degenerate. Wagner's writings have the defect, very general among German writers, and conspicuous in Max Nordau, of being verbose. They all make us crave for "Der langen Rede, kurzen Sinn."

The fundamental idea in Wagner's great work—"The Art Work of the Future"—is that the arts should co-operate, and that each individual art should attain to its perfection in conjunction with other arts. Max Nordau in no way disproves the soundness of this view by saying that "Goethe's lyric poetry and the 'Divina Commedia'" need no landscape painting, that "Michael Angelo's 'Moses' would hardly produce a deeper impression surrounded by dancers and singers," and that "the 'Pastoral Symphony' does not require a complement of words in order to exercise its full charm."

With that logic peculiar to Max Nordau, he quotes a passage from Schopenhauer in which this thinker mildly deprecates such co-ordination of the arts as was to be found in the operas of his time, and our alienist wishes us to accept this as a proof of insanity in Wagner's admiration for the opera. He forgets the important fact that Wagner's greatness is proved by the way in which he has succeeded in obliterating at least the worst defects of the opera as it existed before him, and that he has rendered it a complete and harmonious expression of combined and elevated arts. The quoted passage from Schopenhauer could be no condemnation of Wagner's operas as it was written before they saw the light. In the operas, as they used to be, there was much that tended to disturb the imagination and even to arouse laughter. The most exasperating incongruities were indulged in. An exciting hunting chorus would be played and sung while two rows of lady supers would walk in from each side of the wings in Indian file, each bearing as a hunting implement a yard-long piece of wood surmounted by a piece of tin. The impossible dresses, the demure demeanour, the solemn faces, the absurd lances—carried like candles in a nuns' procession—all this clashed so terribly with the music and the theme as to suggest a burlesque. A band of conspirators afraid of being detected, yet shouting at the top of their voices some compromising chorus; a man with a deadly wound rising to his feet and singing a lively and complicated aria; a messenger in the hottest haste delivering a message in a slow and long-drawn recitative; an intensely modern consumptive lady dying amid ancient surroundings, trilling in her last gasps musical complexities, during a quarter of an hour, with a marvellously strong and healthy voice —such, and many other absurdities, disfigured the opera before Wagner and Gounod, and well deserved the condemnation of Schopenhauer.

Wagner's assertion that the natural evolution of each art leads to the surrender of its independence and to its fusion with other arts is looked upon by Max Nordau as delirious. To prove this he falls back on biology, and points out that nature develops from the simple to the complex, that originally similar parts develop into separate organs of different structure and independent functions. Why on earth should there necessarily be an analogy between the growth of plants and animals, and between the development of the arts? Any other writer who had been unfortunate enough to indulge in such profound mysticism would certainly have been condemned by Max Nordau to the lunatic asylum. Even if we admit the analogy as permissible, he gains very little by it : for when he speaks of nature as always proceeding from the simple to the complex he describes exactly the development of the arts into the opera—music, poetry and dancing representing each the simple, and the opera representing the complex. What would Max Nordau think of a mad doctor who based his verdict of insanity on such reasoning.

The attentive student of Max Nordau's impeachment of Wagner cannot fail to see that, despite all his efforts to brand him as a degenerate, he has only succeeded in throwing the grand power of that genius into bolder relief. Instead of inducing us to look upon Wagner as a sign of degeneration, he has impressed us with the fact that Wagner's work constitutes an awakening from the slumber in which Philistinism and conventionalism have so long enwrapped humanity, and opened a new vista for the ennobling mission of the arts.

While we must reject Max Nordau's clinging to that pedantry and conventionalism which limits the mission of the arts to the production of isolated pictures for public galleries and the salons of modern Mæcenases, statues for public places, and compositions of *Kammer-musik* for drawing-rooms, we at the same time do not believe that the opera, even as regenerated by the genius of a Wagner, is the highest expression of the arts. There will come a day when the illusions of the stage will be realities, when we shall dispense with the dusty sceneries, the garish footlights, the painted faces, the prudish trappings, which go to make up the mirage which heralds an ideal future. The arts, instead of being relegated to the nursery in order to make room for science, as Max Nordau prophesies, will become its aim. When science has given us health, strength, and beauty, an extended power over nature's forces, when it has solved the terrible social problem on the basis of liberty and progress, then will science be the handmaiden of the arts. Then will the answer be granted to the poet's prayer:

> "Oh! for a muse of fire that shall ascend
> The highest heaven of invention;
> A kingdom for a stage; princes to act;
> And monarchs to behold the swelling scene!"

The arts, after having demonstrated in the opera their solidarity and their independence, will leave that artificial shelter and take up their abode in our homes and in our civic buildings, in our streets, and in our public places, in our arenas and in our temples.

A new renaissance lies ahead of us, and we are all struggling to reach it. The man who thinks and writes, the artist who paints or composes, the peasant at the plough, the miner in the bowels of the earth, all are contributing to further the advent of a new era when the life, the work, the pleasure and the worship of a regenerate race shall be exalted by the arts, and present a realization of what Wagner dreamed while he created.

CHAPTER IX

THE RELIGION OF SELF

THE term egomania is a welcome present from the scientists, which enriches our language with a verbal representation of a psychological condition which is certainly characteristic of our time. We trust that Max Nordau's diagnosis of the disease will be carefully studied by its victims, especially by those who are in the stage where it appears as egoism, self-sufficiency, indifference to others, to society, to the State, and as that fashionable and superior pessimism which despairs of self as an excuse for despairing of others. For, though Max Nordau goes very minutely into the psychological aspect of egomania without indicating its origin or the remedies against it, he evidently does not reject the theory, which seems constantly to be confirmed by actualities, that mental diseases may be fostered and aggravated both by those who suffer from them, as well as by surrounding circumstances.

Putting his opinion as a psychologist together with

that of others, we seem authorized to hope that when our egotistical pessimists have learned that the aristocratic characteristic on which they pride themselves is the beginning of a mental disease, they will fly to such remedies as may be found in the study of useful science and healthy work.

Such authors as Théophile Gautier, Baudelaire, Rollinat, and others, attract especially Max Nordau's attention; but he deals with them in order to show that they individually had degenerated into egomaniacs, and he does not once try to realize the relation between their so-called degeneracy and the general tendencies of our time. Had he done so, he might have felt inclined to be less hard on these exponents of *fin de siècle* corruption. Speaking of the hints which this school of poets and writers sometimes throws out that they are not quite serious, Max Nordau comes very near to discovering their significance when he says about Baudelaire that perhaps "he sought to make himself believe that, with his Satanism, he was laughing at the Philistines." But Max Nordau does not follow up the cue he has thus accidentally dropped upon, but adds a sentence revealing the one-sidedness of his inquiry, when he says: "but such a tardy palliation does not deceive the psychologist, and it is of no importance for his judgment."

That may be so. But it is of the utmost importance to humanity. That the yielding to the promptings of "unconsciousness," to the dictates of instincts bad or good, was on the part of the so-called Parnassians an experimental plunge in the dark—a challenge to those who pretended to know better to show them that they were wrong—cannot be denied by any one who has read their writings with some knowledge of the French character.

These men took up literature at a time when the world began to perceive that science could not satisfy its emotional aspirations, that it could not explain the mysteries of the Universe, or bring about that balance between our emotional and intellectual natures on which a healthy life depends. But this was not the only disillusion which humanity experienced at that time. All the hopes which the altruistic feeling had prompted us to base on democratic governments and scientific political economy had vanished. When the Utopias of the economists turned out to be a *fata morgana,* instead of the solid ladder leading up to the material heaven promised by the religion of humanity of the scientists, a Babylonian confusion arose among the people who had first been told to worship at the shrine of religion, then at the shrine of science, and now stood without any shrine whatsoever In France, more than in any other country, we meet with people whose minds are too subtle and whose emotions are too genuine to permit them to dwell contented in that Philistinism which leans on the one side towards the scientific creed or absence of creed, in order to appear modern, and, on the other side, on religion, in order to be safe, but whose real shrine is the money-safe. These French people, mostly authors and artists, had studied both the religious and the scientific theories, and had found the causes of their miscarriage.

The Church had said, "Nature is vile, man is naturally bad, instincts are prompted by the devil, and knowledge is one of the snares of hell." But the Roman Church had not only failed in its mission to keep up the faith and render humanity virtuous and happy, but was responsible for great social troubles, superstitions, and obstacles to progress. It had good intentions, but the way in which it tried to carry them out rendered them valueless. It required power first, much power, complete power over everything, and the acquisition of power did more harm than the Church could do good when ever so powerful. The Protestant Churches in France were gloomy, prudish, anti-artistic, and appealed with difficulty to any French character. Their dogmas seemed incompatible with scientific truth, and their mission appeared to be rather to persuade their members that they were perfect than to render them perfect. Besides, a great many minds throughout the world, accredited with scientific accomplishments, had mercilessly opposed dogmatic religion.

Science, in its turn, when asked, Where is truth? Where is the ideal? could only point to a pile of facts laboriously built up like a brick wall, and had to confess that what it wished to give instead of religion was mere speculations. The ultimate conclusion it pointed to was selfishness, personal irresponsibility, and a mere animal existence. It failed entirely to satisfy the great moving power in the scheme of humanity—emotions—and could not therefore satisfy human yearnings and aspirations.

The postulates of religion — the wickedness of nature and of man—were rejected as groundless, and the guidance of intellect and science was spurned because they were powerless to influence the emotions.

Finding themselves in the plight of a ship driving about in the ocean without compass or rudder, the Parnassians, the Decadents, and many others, thought it was time to try a desperate course. Perhaps, after all, they thought, nature is good, perhaps human instincts may be trusted; let us be natural and follow our instincts. There was much to encourage the new departure. It had often been found that the purest joys were the most lasting, that the good was the most beautiful, that lives and actions prompted by the altruistic feelings best satisfied selfish yearnings, that vice was disappointing, unhealthy, degrading, and joy-killing; that virtue improved life, increased the capacity for enjoyment, and beautified mind and body. These observations encouraged the belief in the religion of self. The *Ego* was not bad; but it required freedom to develop itself.

Like all founders of systems and philosophies, the Parnassians and Decadents sought for confirmation of their theories in the possibility of a Utopia. In imagining a state of things under which the self should have unlimited latitude for self-realization, where man could satisfy his highest aspirations and enjoy the greatest possible happiness under the guidance of his altruistic promptings, where his instincts should be so sharpened and developed as to unfailingly select the greatest and the most lasting, and therefore the noblest pleasures—in imagining such a state of things these experimentalists perceived that society, such as it was around them, offered thousands of obstacles to every attempt at practical realization of their theories. They thus came to look upon themselves as at war with society, its old standards, its prejudices, its religions, and its morals.

Their writings were at once weapons, challenges, rallying-cries. They were intended to deride, to shock, and to draw attention to the new philosophy. The distinction between good and bad was obliterated.

The artist and the poet should henceforth express their true feelings and nought else. Instinct should take the place of principles. The devil might be worshipped as well as God. Art should have no other object than art. Nature might be abhorred as well as loved. And so on.

From this moral chaos the self was to rise in all its glory. For the present it was distorted by surrounding circumstances. The ugliness and morbidness of the subjects they wrote about and the distortion of their own feelings were the proofs of the decayed state upon which humanity had entered. Characters such as Huysman's Duc des Esseintes were intended to illustrate what the present state of society was, and what its present tenets would lead to. He is intended to represent the final result of our civilization, and to show that disgust of our race may be so great as to inspire a man with the belief that by fostering evil and creating criminals he does a good action in so far as he accelerates the destruction of society.

The Parnassians and the Decadents have no proclaimed creed or any programme, and their own opinion of their philosophy is of the haziest kind. We are therefore far from asserting that we have here interpreted them as they would interpret themselves. Whatever may be said of their style and their writings, they have, at least, the merit of being frank and unsophisticated, and we think it must be recognised that, whether they know it or not, they hold themselves up as the "frightful examples" of the chaotic state into which creeds, principles, morals are falling at the end of this century. To us the moral, both of their existence and of their writing, is that the world, and especially France, stands in sore need of better churches, of a better system of philosophy, and better principles of government. These authors have rendered a great service in tearing away the hypocritical mask which society is so anxious to maintain, and thus demonstrating the great need of regenerating agencies.

Of late, England has been considerably influenced by France, and the æsthetic revolt just referred to naturally affected the English, but merely as a faint echo.

When Max Nordau, who correctly points out the connection between the Decadents in France and the extreme æsthetes in England, insinuates that the whole of English society is affected by it, he labours under a wrong impression. We have had here—and we speak purposely in the past tense— a knot of people who have believed, as Max Nordau states, that a work of art is its own aim, that it may be immoral. But, as he himself has stated, the æsthetic awakening in England has forced art almost in the opposite direction. We have had poets who have imitated Baudelaire and other writers of the same class, but these imitators have, by imitating many others, displayed a weakness which debars them from any great influence. There was a time with us when a thoroughly immoral decadence had a spell of influence and created a sickly literature. But the influence of this sham æstheticism is fast vanishing, since its essence has been mercilessly exposed.

While the influence of the Parnassians and Decadents in France was only small, in England the circumstances which produced them have been in existence among us and have produced effects to some extent similar. The struggle between science and religion, the distrust of both, the failure of social panaceas, and the irresistible pushing of the working class against old social barriers, have produced in a great number of educated men a peculiar state of mind which we wish that Max Nordau had noticed. Whether he would have placed those thus affected among his degenerates as egomaniacs it is impossible for us to decide, but there can be little doubt that egoism is the chief characteristic of a new religion, or a new mental disease, which has made large inroads among educated men. It becomes manifest in their pessimism and in their indifferentism. They believe that everything is bad, that the classes are bad, that the masses are bad, that the country is in a bad state, and that everything will finish badly. At the same time they do not care. They will do nothing to avert the coming evils. They hope that none will think them foolish enough to make themselves martyrs. They wish it to be clearly understood that they care only for themselves and that they take no heed of what happens to others. They loathe the working class, and affect a desire to crush them out of existence at one blow. They belong to the few Englishmen who suspect women of vile things, except of course their mothers, sisters, *fiancées*, and wives. They think life hardly worth living, and certainly not worth any special exertions, but their main preoccupation is the state of their health. They study nothing save their own inclinations and cravings and certain excrescences of the most modern literature. Their capacity for hatred is stupendous in its scope but meek in its expression. They claim to enjoy all the benefits of social life without considering themselves obliged to perform any of its duties. They manage to be spendthrifts without being generous, and to be mean without being economical.

But we are strongly averse from classing these social phenomena among the hopeless egomaniacs. They exaggerate their egotism to such an extent as to suggest that they are rather following a foolish fashion than undergoing moral decay, and that the existence of pinchbeck patriots, political charlatans, sham enthusiasts, and professional philanthropists, has frightened them from showing their best side and using their best abilities, and causes them to flout their pessimism and selfishness in every one's face lest they should be taken for one of these.

In spite of their infatuated posing as degenerate egomaniacs, we believe that many of them may be counted upon as part of those elements from which the future regeneration may spring, when the cloud of scepticism has cleared away, and a goal worthy to strive for is discernible.

CHAPTER X

AN ETHICAL INQUISITION

A VERY large part of the sum-total of the work accomplished by Max Nordau in "Degeneration" consists in describing scientifically the psychological phenomena which underlie the idiosyncrasies of certain authors and artists : in giving scientific names to their weaknesses, and in setting forth the relations in which such weaknesses stand to madness. These idiosyncrasies, these weaknesses and their relations to madness were well known to observant people long before Max Nordau's book was written, and to these his work is simply the technical explanation of familiar phenomena. In another chapter we shall dwell at greater length on the difference of views which Max Nordau tends to bring about. Here we wish to point out that, in spite of the mass of scientific phraseology employed by Max Nordau, and in spite of the difference of views he endeavours to bring about, in what seems to be his main object, he is entirely in accord with millions of sound-minded people in this country. We English deplore, as deeply as any one can, the existence of artists and works of so-called art which appeal rather to the morbid than to the healthy mind ; of poetry, novels, and dramas, calculated to flatter the corrupt, instead of stimulating in all a desire for elevation. We especially deplore the diabolical work done by pornographic artists and authors.

Owing to this accord in aims with Max Nordau, his work has been read, and is being read, by thousands in this country, in the hope that his vaunted science and his strong mind would show us the right remedies. But in this respect we have been sorely disappointed ; for instead of meeting with that complete grasp of the subject to which English scientists have accustomed us, we meet in his proposal of remedies with that dazed and superficial logic which throughout his work clashes so strangely with his power of perceiving and of marshalling his facts.

The way he proposes to treat the "mystics, but especially ego-maniacs, and filthy pseudo-realists," forcibly reminds us of the solemn resolution of the rats to bell the cat. He says :—

" Society must unconditionally defend itself against them. Whoever believes with me that society is the natural organic form of humanity, in which alone it can exist, prosper, and continue to develop itself to higher destinies ; whoever looks upon civilization as a good, having value and deserving to be defended, must mercilessly crush under his thumb the anti-social vermin. To him who, with Nietzsche, is enthusiastic over the 'freely-roving, lusting beast of prey,' we cry, 'Get you gone from civilization! Rove far from us! Be a lusting beast of prey in the desert! Satisfy yourself! Level your roads, build your huts, clothe and feed yourself as you can! Our streets and our houses are not built for you; our looms have no stuffs for you; our fields are not tilled for you. All our labour is performed by men who esteem each other, have consideration for each other, mutually aid each other, and who have to curb their selfishness for the general good. There is no place among us for the lusting beast of prey; and if you dare to return to us, we will pitilessly beat you to death with clubs.'"

All this sounds very well; but if Max Nordau believes that in this passage he has given us the true method of how to defend society against its literary and artistic enemies, he labours under a delusion with regard to his own achievements that savours somewhat of megalomania. His big words, his righteous indignation and his manifold signs of exclamation are not a magic wand, are not a Saint Patrick's mitre, with power to banish toads and serpents from the country.

When he says that society should be defended, we

can understand him. But when he says that society must defend itself, he drops into the mist of commonplace and meaningless generalities. The word society stands for one of those things which will serve very well as the object of an activity, but not as a subject, because while its smallest component part may be affected, action is only possible through an organized co-operation of all its parts. To a German who has never witnessed the attempt of a free democratic community to launch out into collective activity, this difference in the active and passive positions of society may never have occurred. To him the activity of society seems an easy matter, because in his mind society is represented by a concentrated, powerful, and pragmatical administration. If Max Nordau had said "government should defend," instead of "society should defend," he would at least have been logical; but this he could not do, because, though an enemy to personal liberty, he has seen enough of German forms of government to reject the postulate of the socialists regarding the infallibility of the central power; while at the same time he has a healthy contempt for the judgment of the continental police. He therefore says that society must defend itself, and thus gives us a gratuitous piece of advice which is thousands of years old.

He calls upon all those who share his views to tell the enemies of their race to be gone from civilization.

But will they go? Why should they be more obedient than the spirits from the vasty deep? The administration of society would have to be completely centralized, and the central government would have to be absolutely despotic, in order to compel such an exodus. Even with such a government it might be extremely difficult to accomplish. The most despotic government in the world—the Russian Government—have encountered enormous difficulties in trying to expel the Jews, and this despite the fact that in this endeavour they had the sympathies of the majority of the Russian people, and could easily ascertain who were Jews and who were not.

A government, in England for example, that would attempt to expel pernicious authors and artists would have none of these facilities. They would first have to pass an Act of Parliament—the Graphomaniac, Egomaniac, Pornographomaniac Authors and Symbolist Artists Expulsion Act—and at least twenty governments would be turned out before it could get passed. But let us suppose that Parliament had decided on such an expulsion of these offenders, then the real difficulties would begin, namely, to decide who should be expelled and who should not. As to killing the returning ones with clubs, this mode of execution being abolished among us, hanging would have to be resorted to—an extremely difficult operation in our days, when the abolition of capital punishment is more and more being considered as one of the first steps towards better ethics.

Max Nordau admits that judges and the police cannot help us. The reason which he gives with regard to Germany—the public contempt in which the judges and police there stand—does not apply in England where our judges are beyond reproach, and the police is a highly respected body, in consequence of being less pragmatical than any police force in the world. Experience in England has given us far stronger reasons for not using the law and the police force against authors and artists. Each time it has been done, the very works intended to be suppressed have gained a popularity and a circulation a thousand-fold greater than if they had been left alone.

Instead of tribunals and police, Max Nordau suggests a body similar to an association in Germany bearing the name "Association of Men for the Suppression of Immorality." As he often deals with his authorities, so he here deals with his model tribunal. He turns round and shows that they are no good. "This association, it seems, pursues disbelief more than immorality," he says. Alas! such is the way with associations of frail men. They are apt to leave undone those things which they ought to have done, and to do those things which they ought not to have done. Max Nordau here ranges himself with the crowd of sentimental socialists who are so angry with the world because it cannot see how easily the regeneration of humanity would become by means of an infallible and almighty government. He and they cannot see that this infallible and almighty government is the very thing beyond our reach. If he had inquired logically into the causes of the disappointing results produced by the "Association of Men," he could not have failed to notice that they were more logical than himself. This "Association of Men," wanting to suppress vice by forcible action, exactly as Max Nordau would, were sensible enough to strike at the causes and not at the effects. They had found that atheism, and even free-thinking, generally coincided with immorality; and that on the other hand religious men were generally moral. Consequently, atheism was found to produce immorality, and religion morality. In upholding religion, therefore, they were upholding morality in a most effective way, because morality without religion, or at least without expressed religion, is found only in men of great intellectual powers and scientific attainments; and to educate the mass of the people to that point is, and will for a long time be, out of the question. Religion, therefore, was the only choice of Max Nordau's "Association of Men"; and, if it was right to coerce people into morality, it was surely right to coerce them into religion. From this it should be clear that the fault does not lie in the reasoning of this "Association of Men," but in the postulate which Max Nordau has approved—namely, the coercion of anybody by an "Association of Men."

He expects the new "Society for Ethical Culture" in Berlin to do better, and wishes it to constitute itself as the voluntary guardian of the people's morality. What an extraordinary idea! One set of men guarding the morality of another set of men—a small minority, unauthorised, unrecognised and devoid of all physical power, to guard the morality of the great majority! The London authorities could tell Max Nordau a great deal about the effects of such attempts, even when the guardians of morality have the law and police at their back. But he need not come to London to learn what guarded morality is worth, and what the results of such guardianship are. The history of every country teems with illustrations of the fact that every attempt to coerce the people morally, or physically, into a moral life has invariably brought about more hypocrisy, more secret corruption, and a tone of greater immorality. If he distrusts universal experience, then he ought to know, as a psychologist, that, so long as the human mind and the human emotions are what they are, repression, supervision, and outside interference with personal liberty must demoralize.

The composition of his society would be no guarantee whatever against deplorable effects. He proposes that it should consist of instructors, professors, authors, members of Parliament, judges and high functionaries. To begin with, authors could not be included, because they could not judge and be judged at the same time; and if the qualification of authors were sufficient, what would prevent authors of the Zola type from predominating in the association? Here, as with regard to original causes, Max Nordau fancies that he has struck solid ground when he has removed the difficulty a stage further back. The association is simply an instrument. All depends upon who forges it. Of this he says not a word. He evidently expects it to arise as a miracle like the infallible government of the socialists. Were the German Emperor to select the members of the association—which in Germany he would have to do directly or indirectly—he would take upon himself an enormous responsibility, for the fulfilment of which he would have to acquire the necessary information and the necessary means. He would simply be to ethics what the Pope is to the Catholic religion.

Max Nordau boldly asserts that such an association would have "the power to exercise an irresistible 'boycot.'" Why? He evidently thinks so because his association would be an influential one. He clearly does not know what ought to be an axiom to any one who meddles with social questions; namely, that the circulation of a condemned book increases in an inverse ratio to the respect which the condemning authorities enjoy. Thus, if his association were to consist of nobodies and were to condemn a book, the condemnation would only increase the circulation a little; but if it were to consist of the leading men of the German Empire, the condemned book would be read all over the world. In the matter of public censors nothing is of any avail that is not absolutely despotic. By allowing government and police to exercise all kinds of violence, isolated newspaper paragraphs and leaders can be suppressed before they are published, and the open circulation of condemned books may be prevented. But once the public get hold of the contents of an article and the name of a book, a secret circulation at once sets in. Eye-witnesses who were in France when the French Government confiscated and prohibited Edmond About's "La Question Romaine" can relate the eagerness with which this book was read, and tell of the numbers of copies circulated secretly. We cite this example from the Continent, as it corroborates what always happens in England.

Max Nordau fondly imagines that the judgment

of his association would absolutely "annihilate" not only the book, but the author. The contrary would happen. As long as there is a grain of love of liberty in humanity, the condemnation by an authority of a man's book will make him the object of public sympathy. When Max Nordau says that "no respectable bookseller would keep the condemned book, no respectable paper would mention it," his meaning entirely depends on his standard of respectability—one of those standards he absolutely refuses to give us. Every one knows that there are respectable booksellers and papers, and that there are non-respectable booksellers and papers. But who could undertake to draw the line of demarcation between the two categories? In a small German town where there are only one or two booksellers this line is easily drawn. But how about places like Berlin, Hamburg, Paris, Vienna and London? Besides, a bookseller and a newspaper might be highly respectable, but differ diametrically from an association which would have Max Nordau's approval. Surely he would not push his mania so far as to deny a respectable character to all the booksellers and newspapers who, for instance, refuse to boycot Ibsen?

Max Nordau also thinks that the specialists in insanity should come out of their shells and publicly denounce the degenerate authors and artists. In England, for example, he thinks that Maudsley could exercise a healthy influence. But he would be surprised at the small number of people in England, outside the profession, who read works on mental disease. "Degeneration" has been widely read; but this is because it levels startling accusations against well-known authors and artists, and because it purports to give a novel scientific interpretation of familiar phenomena, with the purpose of turning our opinions with regard to some branches of art and literature topsy-turvy. It is not to science alone that it owes its wide circulation, but to the clever —conscious or unconscious—sophistries it contains. English psychologists and specialists in insanity could not afford to launch out after the manner of Max Nordau. They might secure a certain number of readers; but they would lose their patients. A specialist who came before the public with Max Nordau's artless and ill-considered scheme for the defence of society against its enemies, could not hope to be taken seriously by an English public. In England we have had a too large experience of books with a tendency, of log-rolling, of veiled advertisement, and of sly party thrusts, to be influenced by such a suggestion of lunacy against political opponents as is contained in the following sentence from Max Nordau: "A Maudsley in England, a Charcot, a Magnan in France, a Lombroso, a Tonnini in Italy, have brought to vast circles of people an understanding of the obscure phenomena in the life and the mind, and disseminated knowledge which would make it impossible in those countries for pronounced lunatics with the mania for persecution to gain an influence over hundreds of thousands of citizens."

It is impossible for us to imagine an English specialist in insanity attributing the absence of antisemitism in England to his own writings, or those of other psychologists, as Max Nordau does in this sentence. If the German electors can believe such a wild party distortion, they are not the men we take them for. We have already explained the causes of the existence of anti-semitism in Germany, and of its absence in England. We do not expect that Max Nordau will acknowledge our view to be right. For had he not been so entirely the creature of prejudice on this, as on many other subjects outside his speciality, he would, unassisted, have discovered so obvious a truth.

Englishmen are not less anxious than he to defend society against its enemies; but only the most inexperienced and illogical Englishman would recommend such remedies as our alienist seems to consider as the height of wisdom. Though we have been slow about it, we seem at last to have grasped the not very hidden truth that if society—that is to say, the people—is moral enough to elect an association capable of acting as an ethical censor over art and literature, we believe the people also capable of exercising that censorship directly, instead of indirectly, through an association. This censorship by the people themselves has the immense advantage of working unostentatiously and silently, and without advertising the very work that should be suppressed.

We think it futile to condemn, or even to suppress, a work; and on grounds of expediency only, regardless of principle, to club the sinning author. The source from which the condemned work sprang would yield more such works, and the circumstances which had produced the objectionable author would produce more objectionable authors. These, as well as their works, are the symptoms of a social malady, and we should treat them as such. We have ceased to apply to society the old methods, long since abandoned by the medical profession, of curing an evil by means of violent suppression of the symptoms —methods adhered to by Max Nordau with regard to society, but, let us hope, not with regard to his patients.

We leave the symptoms alone : for they allow us to diagnose the evil, and we go for the causes. In looking for them, we try to keep our minds free from such prejudices as influence Max Nordau's logic. We should not cry out for new ethical standards, for new and impossible moral authorities, while we ruthlessly destroy a standard and an authority—religion—the practical usefulness of which could not be replaced for centuries by any new standard or authority, even if invented now.

Recognising the truth in Voltaire's flippant saying, that if God did not exist we should have to invent Him, we do not, as the superstitious scientists do, first abolish Him and then re-invent Him in the clumsy form of a "mechanical causality." We let the holders of the ominous rings—of which Nathan der Weiser told Saladin—do their utmost to prove by virtue and happiness that they hold the magic ring conferring these privileges. It matters little to us whether the genuine ring be the Christian one, the Jewish one, or the scientists', so long as the belief in the holders of each of the rings stimulates them to prove its genuineness. We would not tell the great majority who pin their faith to the Christian ring—even if we believed it to be spurious—that we can prove it to be worthless, and that the scientist's ring alone will bring salvation: for we know that this ring is beyond the reach of most of them, and that, handled in the wrong way, it will work curses instead of blessings. We limit ourselves to telling them that the rings held by the others must not be despised until the Great Competition is adjudicated.

In our quest for the causes of degeneration, we do not begin by trying to discover traces of lunacy in a small number of prominent citizens. We bear in mind that these are either isolated cases, or types of a generally prevailing tendency. In the first case, we leave them alone; in the second, we search for the cause of this tendency. If we find that the tendency, let us say, towards hysteria, or egomania, in the upper classes is being produced by a craving for excitement, unhealthy pleasures, or artificial sensations, and by a frivolous and empty life, we set about to discover the causes of this craving and this empty life.

If we again discover that the cause is found in the decay of the beliefs in personal responsibility, in the importance of philanthropy, morality, and patriotism, we try to discover why these beliefs have decayed. If it be found that they have decayed simultaneously with and in consequence of the decay of the authority of the Church, we try either to strengthen the influence of the Church by purifying and reforming it, or we replace its dogmas and its doctrines by a healthy and moral philosophy.

Should we find, on the other hand, that the deplorable state among the poorer classes—their suffering, their degradation, and their joyless lives, co-existing with large fortunes, and irremediable under present laws and institutions—leads to the conclusion that the altruistic feelings of the wealthy are useless, and thus prompt among the upper classes selfishness and egomania, and the determination to drown their higher emotions in a giddy life, and in the poorer classes to foster destructive tendencies and the desire for revenge, we turn our attention to social remedies.

No one can turn his attention to the social state of the working-class in England, and throughout the world, without discovering a host of motors active in the production of dire misery, and all the mental and moral degradation that follows in its train—a degradation which aggravates the misery, and reacts, as we have shown, on the upper classes. Nothing will more actively stay the progress of any mental degeneration which might be going on than the removal of the causes of the awful misery suffered by such an alarming proportion of civilized humanity. Max Nordau's warning against mental decay and progression towards folly will, we hope, quicken, if not the higher emotions, at least the sense of self-preservation among the leading classes throughout the world. But it must be regretted that he, not only in his suggestions of remedies, but in many other parts of his work, displays a lack of logic and a want of clear perception as soon as he quits the narrow precincts of his special science and the teachings of his manifold authorities, and falls back on his own reasoning powers. Had he prevented his prejudices from colouring his views, and had he not sacrificed logic for brilliancy, his work would have been of no slight assistance to those who are helping on humanity in its staggering onward movement.

CHAPTER XI

VIGOROUS AFFIRMATIONS

IT has come to our knowledge that a great number of people in this country who have read through the whole of Max Nordau's bulky volume have carried away an impression far from pleasant. Indeed, there are few men or women in a country like England who might not, on some plea or another, come under the suspicion of mental degeneration, if all that Max Nordau says were, regardless of his contradictions, accepted as true. In this country education and morality are based entirely on religious principles, and most of the inhabitants are, either by faith or by dint of sincere philosophical inquiry, to some extent religionists. All these might think themselves included among those whom Max Nordau stigmatises as degenerates. There is also a great number who admire intensely Burne Jones, Rossetti, and many other painters of the same school, and all these have been told, with somewhat brutal frankness, that they are on the road to lunacy. The pieces of Ibsen have a great number of admirers who have welcomed with pleasure the additional intelligence and interest which he has infused into the drama, and who consequently have been pointed out as degenerate imbeciles.

In the light of these facts there remain few educated persons among the upper classes of this country about whose intellectual soundness Max Nordau's work might not raise doubts. This all the more so as his few reservations with regard to people who have demonstrated their sanity by practical ability to conduct their own affairs, sink into insignificance among his voluminous and wholesale accusations, especially as such reservations are forgotten almost as soon as they are made.

This wholesale issue of certificates of madness would not have mattered so much if his work did not carry with it a certain power of conviction which tells especially with the weak, uninstructed mind, and with people who have not read his work with special attention. In fact, we know cases of people of sensitive mind who imagine that, thanks to Max Nordau's book, their friends will look upon them as on the road to lunacy.

There can be little doubt that the strong impression the book has made, sometimes in one way and sometimes in another, is largely due to the style adopted by its author. The secret of this style is revealed in the chapter "Prognosis," where he describes with somewhat elephantine humour the effects in the twentieth century of the present progressing degeneration. He says, among other things, that companies of men will be formed who " by vigorous affirmations are charged to tranquillize persons afflicted with the mania of doubt, when taken by a fit of nervousness."

Such a piece of prophecy could only enter the head of a man who has had practical experience of the great effect produced on nervous people by vigorous affirmations, and, having had this experience, Max Nordau fills his volume with such " vigorous affirmations." His method has succeeded all the better as he evidently belongs to that class of powerful and strong-willed men who, when once they have formed an opinion, hold to it tenaciously, and count as nothing any conviction against their will.

Having followed Max Nordau through his vigorous crusade against that score of people whom he regards as dangerous enemies to humanity, and having pointed out a host of his logical errors, erroneous perceptions, unsound postulates, and exaggerated representations, we propose before closing this volume to examine some of the reasoning methods which give him his apparent strength.

It is to him of great moment that his readers shall not believe in the existence of the thinking and feeling *Ego* as a person, apart from the organic mechanism which conveys impressions and presentations to the *Ego*. He uses all the arguments which that school of thinkers to which he belongs has piled up in order to show that mind is a condition of matter. He says nothing about the arguments on the other side, but treats them as the science of the past. He takes for granted, without showing a vestige of doubt, that human beings are nothing but organic mechanisms. He does not even refer to, or allow that there is, anything beyond the present scientific discoveries, and scornfully ignores the existence of what less prejudiced scientists call the Unknowable. He thus treats a question which still trembles in the balance as if it were already decided in favour of his pet theories.

The attitude which biologists and psychologists take up as such, and with the special purpose of proceeding in their investigations with perfectly unbiassed minds, Max Nordau assumes as a philosopher, and tries to persuade himself and others that he has taken his stand on absolute facts. Science proceeds on the supposition that only that is true which has been proved so by demonstrations to our senses, or through deductions from such demonstrations. This, of course, is a postulate the illogicality of which most scientific men are aware of, and is adopted mostly for the purpose, as it were, of clearing the ground. To assume, apart from their investigating attitude, that there is nothing more to know than what is already known, would be an utterly absurd assumption, as it would, if acted upon, preclude further investigation.

Max Nordau does not, and would not, deny that there is more to learn, but he persists in the view that all future knowledge will be on the lines of our present knowledge, and never contradictory to the present prevailing scientific dogmas. He remains under this impression, because he forgets that science has progressed, progresses, and, as far as we see now, always will progress through investigations by our senses, and that this fact brings two important truths conspicuously into relief. The first, that our senses are liable to deceive us, and that consequently the difference between primitive views—the result of imperfect observation—and the scientific opinions of the day, is not one of kind, but simply one of degree. In olden times the senses deceived us very much, and nowadays they deceive us less. But to what an extent they deceive us now the future alone can reveal. The second, that science with the present methods cannot investigate anything that does not appeal to our senses.

To deny the existence of anything that does not appeal directly to our senses is absurd, because we should have to deny all the forces of nature. The existence of these can only be detected by their effects. The more science teaches us about forces, the more the view gains adherence that the forces are not a state of matter, but a thing apart, if matter is not a state of force. Even if this view should prove to be correct, the error it would dispel, that force is a state of matter, would be pardonable, as force has only come within the perception of our senses through its effect on matter.

Psychology has to some extent succeeded in tracing and in describing certain forces which are at work in our nerves and our brains, such as, for example, reveal themselves in the reception and elaboration of presentations. But within every human being there are well-known phenomena which tell of forces — or of one general force — which so far have escaped all investigation. These phenomena are emotion, judgment, will.

Attentive readers of Max Nordau's book will have noticed that, in his scientific dissertations on the actions of the brain, these factors—emotion, judgment, will — turn up suddenly without the slightest explanation as to whence they come and what they are, though they seem to completely determine the action of the whole organism. It is with this enormous gap in their chain of reasoning that some scientists, with more learning than logic, jump to the conclusion that the thinking and feeling *Ego* is only a state of matter.

Max Nordau, being anxious, as we have already mentioned, to magnify the importance of his psychological theories by undermining his readers' belief in the existence of anything unscientifically called "soul" or "spirit," renders his task easier by attacking religion, of which the belief in the existence of the spiritual *Ego* is a vital part. He knows that if he can compass the rejection of the idea of religion he kills two birds with one stone. He gets rid of the personal *Ego* as well as the belief in eternal life, both of which, if admitted to be realities, would strongly point to an intelligent Providence, the existence of which would be a colossal impediment to the glorification of science and of scientists.

The way in which he strives to undermine religious belief is ingenious and often effective. He trusts chiefly to the historical argument. He goes back to primitive man in order to show that he, in his ignorance of nature, attributed those natural phenomena which strongly impressed him to some man mightier than himself. Max Nordau tries to show that out of this belief arose what he would call superstition, the several forms of religion. He here of course appeals to feeling more than to reason. People do not like to feel that they have remained in the depth of ignorance of the primitive savage, and might feel disposed to join the glorious company of the apostles of science. But if we use our reasoning powers, we cannot fail to perceive that science has merely taught us the methods by which, and the laws according to which, nature works, and that as to the forces behind the laws of nature the scientist is as ignorant as the primitive savage.

Max Nordau also pursues that diplomatic course —or commits the error—as we have already pointed out, of confounding religion with the Churches. It is easy to inspire distrust in religion if it be permitted to consider Pope Borgia, Ignatius Loyola, and Dr. Stöcker as its inevitable results. By analyzing and to some extent distorting the essence of ritual, Max Nordau seeks to point out that Christian worship is not only sheer imbecility, but also an insult to the supposed God. He never notices such discrepancies between the Churches and religion as are, for example, revealed by the anti-semitist movement in Germany, which naturally he keenly resents. From the defects, the shortcomings, the superstitions, the antiquated dogmas of the Churches, he tries to draw the sweeping conclusion that a belief in an intelligent Providence, in the existence of a soul, and in a spiritual life independent of the body, is the outcome of degenerate mental powers.

The views that by such means he endeavours to impose upon his readers mean that man, being an organic mechanism, ceases to exist when he dies. If this be so, there is no personal responsibility, and only that man would be wise, rational, undegenerate who so arranges his life that he may live long, keep in good health, and enjoy all the pleasures that he desires, be they noble or ignoble. To test, then, whether a man who is, who believes he is, or merely poses as, a disbeliever in future responsibility, we ought to examine how he regulates his life. Only in this manner can we discover to what an extent he is influenced—to use Max Nordau's own language—by the inherited tendencies to worship, lurking somewhere in the innermost recesses of his consciousness, or, to use our own language, by the instinctive feeling of personal responsibility which has characterized humanity in every stage of barbarism and civilization.

The fact that a great many scientists, including Max Nordau, do not live as if they were perfectly convinced of the non-existence of personal responsibility beyond the grave, requires quite a different kind of explanation than that generally afforded, before we abandon the belief that they are self-deceivers. The moral scientists themselves have found the necessity of some explanation, and this is what they say, though perhaps in other words:

"We do not believe in any responsibility beyond the grave, but we do what we think our duty to humanity. We should be sorry and ashamed to be actuated by a fear of punishment or the desire for reward, and not to do what is right and good for the sake of the right and the good."

This sounds very beautiful, but too boastful almost to be accepted as the bare truth. Some of them who are aware of this, or who are genuinely too modest to thus stand forward as demi-gods, add, " In living and acting as we do, and wanting others to live and to act in the same way, we are not more unselfish, nor morally better, than others. We are only wiser; in fact, more intellectually selfish. And all we desire of other people is that they should be intellectually selfish. In exercising self-control and devotion to others, we do not deprive ourselves of pleasures and enjoyments, because most of these come to us from our surroundings and from society at large. For what we do for our wives and families we get love in return; for what we do for society and the race, we get two rewards: firstly, esteem and reputation, perhaps money; and, secondly, all the social advantages which are valuable to us in the same proportion as society is in a healthy state."

This seems highly convincing, but it does not by far cover the whole ground. Whoever has studied our times well knows that a man can secure for himself, and even for his family and friends, enormous advantages by disregarding and violating the interests and moral rights of others, and also that, when wholesale rascality succeeds, when it is productive of great wealth, great social and political power, it also secures esteem and reputation. There are, of course, men in positions, the stock-in-trade of which consists in honesty and even philanthropy; but there are others, and millions of them, who could, under the present social systems of the world, amass fortunes and rise to distinction by systematic robbery. Thousands of cases could be stated in proof of the fact that, in the absence of the belief in responsibility after death, selfishness will prompt men to hurt their fellow-beings and society in order to secure money, power and reputation for themselves. Take the case of a poor labourer who, in the usual course, will work and suffer during his whole life and die in poverty. To escape such a destiny many roads are open to him if he have courage, exceptional ability, and no belief in a hereafter. He could commit a variety of crimes in order to give him a start in life without the slightest chance of being detected, and without experiencing the smallest inconvenience during his lifetime. He might even avoid violent and vulgar crimes, and operate in a safer manner. He might blackmail a rich man. He might in war betray his country. He might sell himself to a corrupt political party. He might join the army of some selfish sovereign bent on conquest and plunder, and gain a high position. Or he might pursue yet safer methods. He might turn first a usurer, then a financier. He might keep a degrading public-house, or a gigantic immoral place of amusement. He might issue a debasing newspaper, write corrupting books and dramatic pieces. Provided he does not expose himself to the hatred, contempt, and even the unfavourable criticism of his fellow-beings, or injure his health, there is positively nothing to prevent him from adopting all these courses to the great detriment of humanity, so long as he is perfectly sure that he shall not be called to account after death.

What some of our scientists forget is that very few people are in the same position as they themselves are, where respectability and quasi-philanthropy pays; but on the contrary, that the great majority live under the constant temptation to secure wealth, health, esteem, and reputation, by means which are injurious to society. To such arguments they can only reply that the man, however successful, who attains his success by anti-social means runs a risk of ruining the happiness of his life by loss of self-respect.

But, if the man has a conscience,—and he could

not lose his self-respect without one—it could not trouble him so long as he was convinced that he had done the best for himself. By bringing the conscience at all into the discussion, the scientists fall back on an emotion which has been always intimately associated with the sense of personal responsibility, and which they themselves have been compelled, in order to protect their theories, to deny absolutely as an instinct or to represent as the result of religious education.

For this reason, Max Nordau would not call that instinct in man which prompts him to live and act morally—an instinct which is the original motor of all moral progress—conscience. He would probably prefer to call it the social instinct. But names matter little. The essential point is, that there exists in man's consciousness a strong instinct which cannot be reasoned away. This instinct is intimately connected with another, without which it would never have produced the results we see around us—namely, the instinct that the *Ego* is imperishable. No one would deny the universal existence of this instinct, but plenty of scientists, while acknowledging it as an inherited tendency, would deny it any value as an argument in favour of the immortality of the *Ego*, on the ground that a hazy, unreasoned, and utterly inexplicable yearning need not have a distinct goal.

The instinct of human beings is a subject which has been very much neglected by science, and for the good reason that, whatever instincts may be natural to man, they have been carefully smothered by teachings, examples, and experience, all appealing to his reason from infancy upwards. He never uses, never tries, and never suspects the existence of his instincts, and when accidentally they lead him right, he regards the fact as a delusion, and even avoids mentioning it from a fear of being laughed at. This has however not prevented men, and often remarkable men, from being guided by their instincts; only it is called feeling, taste, luck. There are examples of men who owe the greater part of their success to instinctive feeling, and who have committed great mistakes by having trusted too much to it. Besides it is generally believed that woman's instincts are clear and trustworthy, and many men consider themselves to have been largely benefited by consulting them.

But, in order to get at a true appreciation of the value and power of instincts, we must go to the animals. What else but instinct could we call the feeling which allows the carrier-pigeon to find its way from London to Paris in an atmosphere of darkness and fog which would render it impossible for the most experienced mariner to distinguish between north and south. It is a well-known fact that dogs and even cats that have been left behind by their owners have followed them at great distances, though the owner has gone by rail or water and the animal has had to find its way across country. In face of such facts and considerations, no man who has not a strong bias would suggest that an instinct that is general to humanity need not be heeded.

The instinct of personal responsibility cannot be re-christened social instinct and then minimised by the assertion that the social instinct is the outcome of reason, the sense of self-preservation and intelligent selfishness : for in that case the poor labourer who wanted to become wealthy and famous, as instanced above, could be as evil as he liked so long as he was successful, and could not be restrained by the social instinct, but only by conscience, or in other words, the feeling of unlimited personal responsibility.

Atheistic scientists, who lead a moral and useful life, cannot hold themselves up as a pattern of results produced by social instincts, because in the great majority of men, placed differently, these instincts would permit them to injure society to an enormous extent. Nor does the assertion of these scientists bear the stamp of sincerity when they say : " Behold us, we have no belief in personal responsibility beyond the grave. And yet we labour and run risks for the good of humanity. We sacrifice our time, our money, our health for others, and we remain poor, while we could be rich. Our life is the outcome of intelligent selfishness."

They would have a better chance of convincing us, if they said: "Life after death is impossible. We prove by our lives that we believe this. Our moral lives and our humanitarianism are sheer hypocrisy which we practice in order to get esteem and fame. The books we write are not true, but they bring us money, and we do not care how much evil we inflict on humanity by ripping away the only foundation on which its morality and happiness can be built, while the substitute which we supply is worthless. We might have averted an immense amount of vice and degradation by leaving old religions alone until the Religion of Humanity was perfect enough to replace them. But we attack them now because in this way we make money and fame."

It is not the well-meaning, plodding scientist, striving to arrest disease, lessen pain, and dispel superstition, that can bounce us into the belief in personal irresponsibility. This could only be done by real flesh and blood, Ducs des Esseintes, men like the hero in Huysman's novel, "A Rebours." This author, whom Max Nordau classes among drivelling imbeciles, has shown that he has a clearer idea than our clever alienist what type of men the certitude of personal irresponsibility could produce. We are fully convinced that Max Nordau is no Duc des Esseintes at heart, masquerading as a benefactor of humanity, and, if he boasts a little of his good intentions and not at all of his wickedness, it is because he believes that what he does is right, and does it because he is prompted by that strong sense of personal responsibility which his scientific prejudices and his lack of logical power cause him to deny.

Having striven by "vigorous affirmations" to implant the belief in his readers' minds that they have no *Ego* independent of their body, and that they consequently are fatally doomed to become what their defective brains and nerves are bound to make them, he proceeds with another series of " vigorous affirmations," that degeneration is on the increase, that it is characteristic of the end of the century, that the men whom we take for geniuses are mattoids, and finally, that the whole of our western civilization is degenerate. We have, in preceding chapters, tried to show how he has neglected to pay any attention to the many signs all over the civilized world indicating an increase in mental and moral powers; how he endeavours to overwhelm his readers by comparisons between the symptoms in real degenerates, or lunatics, and similar symptoms

—accompanied however by perfect rationality and great intelligence—in authors and artists, and concludes that they are as mad as the madman. He tries to force this conclusion on the unwary reader by simply ignoring all other grounds for eccentricity that would have been taken into account by an unbiassed enquirer.

Let us instance the way in which he judges Zola. He never for an instant regards him as a free agent, but speaks of him as a patient suffering from erotic madness and other brain and nerve affections, which compel the novelist to write, and to write exactly in the vein he does.

The very idea that human beings should be thus subjected to all kinds of irresistible impulses produces the same gruesome impression as the old stories of demoniacal possessions. Max Nordau might as well have described Zola as a man hating above all things the writing of novels, with a natural repugnance for anything savouring of the obscene, compelled by a demon in possession of his body and his soul to write the history of the Rougeon-Maquarts and other distasteful works. On the careful reader the impression would have been precisely the same. But no number of "vigorous affirmations" would have induced even the most weak-minded of readers to have accepted the demon, while Zola's eroticism and his mischievous olfactory nerves may have imprinted themselves upon the minds of some by dint of scientific dissertation.

While it would seem to most people rational to study Zola's character and the state of his mind, in order to form a correct idea of the objects he has in view, Max Nordau, by his method of supposing that a writer is not a free agent, but is compelled to exhibit for the readers of his works the innermost recesses of his consciousness, proceeds in the opposite manner; he evolves the character of writers from the characters of their books. From what he says about Zola, one feels inclined to conclude that this author devotes the large amounts he makes by his writings to the gratification of bestial lusts, living in a kind of harem of degraded women, rapidly destroying by debauch every spark of intelligence left in his tottering brain. We do not know M. Zola personally, but, from what we hear, he seems to live a quiet and laborious life with his wife in a peaceful country house, and far from spending his earnings in riotous living, he banks them as a reserve for old age, to which he seems likely to attain. When however a man's private life and rational attention to his own business seem to clash conspicuously with Max Nordau's diagnoses, his serenity and self-confidence are not in the slightest degree disturbed, because he has given his description to the man's tendency in a "psychiatric sense," and has referred to the man's actual life. But the decrepancy between the author's actual life and the life he, according to Max Nordau, ought to lead, is not an extenuating circumstance in the eyes of so harsh a judge as our alienist. On the contrary, it aggravates the sentence, for if the accused author is not in reality the monster he ought to be, it is simply because his attenuated physique does not allow of it, and drives him to through all his debaucheries in his imagination.

We do not admire such literature as Zola has put forth, and do not believe that it has accomplished one iota of the good at which its author, according to his admirers, aims. But all rational men should bear in mind that such books are sure indications that there is something rotten in the State. To ascertain to what an extent the circumstances surrounding the author are capable of inducing a sound-minded man like Zola to write such books, before jumping to the conclusion that such authors are lunatics, would be the method adopted by sincere searchers after truth.

A rapid survey of the circumstances under which Zola began to write will at once show that the inborn eroticism and even coprolalia which Max Nordau tries to foist upon Zola were not the only influences to which he was subjected. In Paris, as in all great capitals, there is a host of young ambitious *littérateurs* who compete for the attention not only of the public but of the publishers. It is far from certain that the books which most please the public would be most acceptable to the publishers, and the latter are, therefore, to a great extent responsible for the state of literature. Max Nordau says that M. Alphonse Lemerre was able to make Parnassians, as the editor, Cotta, in the first half of the century, made German classics; and he is right. A Parisian publisher has the power to make pornographic authors just as well as Parnassians. He is a business man, and of course wishes to obtain a large circulation for his books, and, therefore, is on the look-out for authors who are sensational one way or another. At the time Zola began to write the obscene novel was beginning to be fashionable. Paul de Kock and his imitators, had become old-fashioned, and the corruption of the Third Empire, as well as the spread of scientific atheism, had created a demand for something racier than the peccadilloes of light-hearted *viveurs*. Besides, pessimism was in the ascendant, and erotic literature had to be morbid instead of gallant and gay.

Several authors of great ability, but strongly influenced by the pessimism of the time, and with the field of their ethical studies limited to the Parisian boulevards and the Quartier Breda, had paved the way for that false realistic literature of which Zola's writing may be called the climax. The publishers, knowing their market, were eager to accept books of an obscene character, provided they were serious and written in a philosophical spirit. Zola may have seen his way to eclipse anything written in that style, and being himself a child of his time,—materialist, and nervously inclined to exaggeration—may have seized upon the chance of making money and fame, though he probably foresaw that his first novels would expose him to the execration of the Philistines and the respectable world. He might also have foreseen that one day he would be able to establish a sufficient fame to be received by English *littérateurs* as a genius of his time. If, therefore, Zola's object was to push himself to the front, in the manner we here suppose him to have done, he has certainly succeeded—a fact which could not establish his intellectual degradation. He simply yielded to a tremendous temptation, and, if he did so under the impression that the scientists had completely proved the non-existence of personal responsibility, Max Nordau should be the last to blame him.

But there is not the slightest necessity to assume —nor do we assume—that Zola yielded to any temptation at all. On the contrary, it is perfectly possible that, in writing the books he has, he sincerely believed that he was serving some good purpose. Knowing how many other Frenchmen feel in this respect, we might well suppose that he reasoned somewhat in the following manner: Religion is wrong, and a fraud practised by the clever on the simple-minded. The control which the Church has assumed over the relations of the sexes is one of the means by which it retains its power, and is fraught with immense unhappiness to the people. The separation of the sexes and the devout decency which refrains from openly speaking or writing about sexual subjects, distorts the people's ideas, inflames their imagination, and tempts them into unhealthy vice. Nature is not sinful. It is either the only divinity we have, or it is created by the Almighty, and in this case it is holy. To yield rationally to its dictates is therefore no sin. Books should therefore be written to prove this point, and at the same time accustom the people to look upon nature and its laws without shame, without hypocrisy, and without running the risk of being overpowered by wild passions. In this way humanity may be elevated, because it will be frank and natural, and religion, which science has proved to be inimical to humanity, will lose its influence.

We are not saying that Zola's ideas ran in this groove, only that it is possible that they did. If they did, he would have been utterly wrong; but he would not have been the first nor the last man whose views have been influenced by their interests. No man who knows both France and England better than Max Nordau seems to do could for one moment doubt that had Zola been born and educated in England, where the surroundings are so vastly different to those of France, he would have written books of quite a different character, and probably free from obscenity. If this be true, it constitutes another reason why the surrounding circumstances of an author should be considered before it is asserted that inborn degeneration is alone responsible for the blemishes of his work.

Max Nordau himself points out that the fashion which brought Zola to the front is on the decline, and that his influence is on the wane. If so, it only proves how limited the influence of such supposed degenerates really is, and that,—at least, with regard to Zola,—Max Nordau's book is out too late, and those who have been deeply impressed by his " vigorous affirmations" about the mental decay of the race need not despond.

Over and over again civilization and society have been threatened by new and apparently dangerous tendencies, but they have generally culminated in absurd exaggerations, and have thus lost their potency. Who knows whether Zola, through the wisdom that the years bring, will not change his opinions, and with them his vein of writing? We feel morally certain that he is now engaged on some novel entirely free from those erotic allusions which Max Nordau says he cannot avoid—a book as pure as the first part of "La Joie de Vivre"; and if he does, what will become of Max Nordau's imperious dogmas?

Another of those features of Max Nordau's work which strongly impresses his readers is seriousness. He speaks throughout in that grave and solemn tone — the So-spake-the-Lord style — which never yet failed to impress superficial readers. He is anxious to convey the impression that if he has to say unpleasant things, it is because his teachings are momentous to humanity, and not because he wishes to be sensational. He condescends to speak about poetry, drama, and music, but he plainly shows it to be his opinion that all these are vanities, and hardly worthy to occupy a great man's thoughts. He aims at crushing with his contempt both artists and poets, the whole herd who have neglected science, and who try to divert the attention of humanity from this all-important subject. He would scare us with the threat that, when science has elevated humanity for a little longer, such frivolities as poetry, music and dancing will be relegated to the nursery. Grown-up men and women, who now indulge in such pastimes, are made to feel that they belong to degenerates, and that they only prove their folly if they look upon themselves with any self-respect. He endeavours to deprive love between persons of the two sexes of its poetical reality, and to wrap it in a gloomy scientific misconception by regarding it as a feeling of comradeship grown out of habit, or as the same sexual instinct as in animals. The pure and real love which permeates life, which gives to man his manhood, and to woman her true womanhood, which has created the home, and therefore the State—this love he denies, and expects serious-minded readers to look upon the world-phenomenon and the drama of humanity deprived of their chief elements — light, heat, and motion. He speaks of the tendency in men and women to take their own life when its burdens outbalance its pleasures as calmly as if suicide were the usual exit from our earthly existence.

Max Nordau thus obtains part of his success by the same methods as those so freely adopted by the gloomy anathematising preachers—rapidly becoming types of the past—who, by threats of the devil and hell fire, aim at compelling their hearers to turn their attention from this world in order to brood exclusively on dismal dogmas. He would fain banish from our minds all that appeals to what is truest within us—our imagination and our emotions—as the kill-joy fanatics in the pulpit have banished from our villages the maypole, the dance on the green, and the forfeit game.

He is much mistaken if he believes that by such means he can in our days produce a lasting impression on the common sense and intensely human English mind. Here and there he may drive some clouded soul into neo-Catholicism, and augment the ranks of the symbolists and the decadents, but he will only make the morbid more morbid, or morbid in a different mood. The hardworking and enlightened Englishman does not apply himself savagely to his business for business sake. Nor does he encourage scientific progress for the sake of science.

When he considers himself, and is considered by others, an eminently practical man, it is because he knows what he aims at, and uses, studies, and encourages the most effective and promptest means to attain his ends. But the secret and the essence of this English practicality lies in the fact that his aims, so clear and so precise, are determined by his imagination, his emotions, and his instincts. Unlike the German who despairs of realizing his ideal, the Englishman has it in his imagination as clearly before him as the architect has the plans, elevations and sections of the palace he is going to build. He does not begin to build until he is convinced that every detail is correct. Nothing discourages him more than the spoiling and blurring of his ideals; he stops his work, as does the builder when his drawings are lost, or found impracticable.

It is vain for Max Nordau to try to persuade the average Englishman, be he educated or not, that the enjoyments which enchant him in his youth shall not cast their roseate hue over the rest of his days. Poetry, music, the drama, are part and parcel of the pleasures the English people look forward to when business has supplied them with the means of enjoying them in the expensive form in which, with us, unfortunately, they are alone obtainable in perfection.

It is not only such enjoyments as educated people of all ages appreciate which for an Englishman retain a life-long charm. Even his boyish tastes give zest to his life, so long as he retains his faculties. At ten years of age he reads, raves and dreams about horses and dogs; at seventy he rides to hounds, and at a still more advanced age he partakes in all the excitements of the racecourse. As a boy he reads about travels and adventures; at middle age, or even later, we find him travelling all over the world in quest of big and small game. Cricket, football, boating, and athletics in general represent the life of English boys, and far into old age they can seldom refrain from glancing at the sporting columns of their paper, which to a foreigner appear as interesting as the dullest of dull market reports; while athletic sports are witnessed by ever-growing crowds of people of all ages, who watch the proceedings with a zest as intense as that of the Spaniard watching a bull-fight.

And to people who thus enjoy their lives, Max Nordau would say: "You are degenerates, because you enjoy childish things. Put them behind you, and rise to my level. Take a seat at the table of science, where we will show you by dissection, and by vivisection, the minutest details of the entrails of those creatures which, in the fulness of their life, in the beauty of their form, afford you a childish delight."

If such be the road to regeneration, only the weak-minded among the English people will enter upon it. Thousands might momentarily experience a depression—a gloom similar to that produced by the fulminating and damnation-dealing preacher one meets with in country districts. The dismal appearance of the orator, his description of hell, of an accursed world, of the narrow way to salvation, as well as the scared faces in the dark and dank little church, may evoke a gruesome mood while the sermon lasts. But on coming out into the summer air, into the midst of the revivifying sunshine, of the rustling trees, radiant flowers, singing birds, dancing butterflies, and softly humming bees, the healthy minded of the congregation experience a sense of relief and joy; for the uncharitable condemnation of the ascetic preacher is powerfully contradicted by the direct and unmistakable language in which nature appeals to man's emotions.

The depressing effect of Max Nordau's book is enhanced by his ostentatious display of knowledge, and by the absolute faith he himself has in it. He follows the methods of wily political speakers. These have a way of piling proofs upon proofs in order to demonstrate the truth of such points as are almost self-evident; and when they have thus established among their audience a confidence in their logic, they slur over the weak points, take for granted that everything is proved, and draw a plausible conclusion devoid of any direct connection with the arguments. A postmaster-general, for example, does not wish to be bothered with the reduction of postage, and, in order to resist such a proposal, he will deliver a lengthy harangue to show that the work of the post-office is useful to the public, that it cannot be well administered without sufficient revenue, the necessity of keeping a complete staff, the impossibility of reducing wages and salaries, and many other points which are perfectly clear without demonstration. He will then suddenly conclude that the post-office works at present with very small means, and that, if those means are further reduced, disorganization and disorder may ensue. To be able to draw this conclusion, he has to take for granted that the reduced postage would mean reduced income to the post-office, while in reality it may mean the very contrary.

In the same way Max Nordau gives us pages upon pages in order to show us such facts as psychological science has established, and then boldly elicits supposed facts which science never has and may never be able to prove. We have already given plenty of instances of this, and they need not be referred to again. His careful minuteness in psychological matters often induces the unwary reader to accept his unproved statements purporting to represent facts drawn from other branches of knowledge. Thus, for example, he speaks of matters pertaining to sociology, economy, administration and politics, as if he were a universally acknowledged authority on these subjects. It will suffice, however, to read his plan for arresting the spread of degeneration to understand at once on what feeble foundations his apparent omniscience rests. His ideas of an ideal social order is an impossible amalgamation of socialistic as well as communistic fallacies. While he retains the absurd postulate of the socialists, that a perfect government could be established, distributing all the wealth of the nation among individuals, he indulges heedlessly in the communistic delusion that those who accumulate under the present system would continue to accumulate wealth at the same rate when the government confiscates all fortunes left by deceased individuals. He does not see that people under such a system would take very good care to dispose of their property before they die, a course which even the German police could not prevent.

He does not insist on these errors, but they come out distinctly as indispensable links in the association of ideas, underlying his views regarding the anti-semitist movement, the dangers of individual liberty, the bestial propensities of the masses, and the necessity of a government composed of strong-minded scientific men. It is only too easy to see that in all his suggestions of working out the terrestrial paradise of humanity,—which one day, according to him, will be the outcome of science,—he is guided entirely by prejudice and feeling. In summing up what he has said on this subject, his ideal social order presents itself to our minds as unfree, completely subjected but well-cared-for masses benevolently governed by senates of strong-minded, scientifically educated men—the Jews.

The gloom and unrest called forth by Max Nordau's work in nervous minds no doubt gain in strength from the apparently powerful personality behind it. But it suffices, as we have shown, to divest this imposing giant of his assumed power in order to escape from his influence. Max Nordau, had he not done so before, reveals himself unmistakably in the very last sentence of his book as one largely beset by human frailties when, in self-glorification, he quotes the words of Him whose work he so strenuously attempts to undermine and oppose. In order to assure his readers that his object, as a scientist, is to benefit humanity, to lead it further on the road on which religion, so much contemned by him, has already taken it some distance, he quotes Christ's words: "Think not that I have come to destroy the law or the prophets; I have not come to destroy, but to fulfil."

We here refrain from the temptation to write half a dozen pages in order to show, in Max Nordau's own manner, how, by quoting from the Scriptures, by appealing to faith and emotion, by comparing himself to Christ, he is symbolic with Paul Verlaine, he is mystical with the neo-Catholics, he is emotional with Rossetti, he is an egomaniac with the Diabolists and a melogomaniac with Wagner. But we refrain, and only say that he is human.

CHAPTER XII

REGENERATION

IF the manifold discussions which have raged around the question of human progress have failed to establish a consensus of opinion, it is largely due to the absence of any exact definition of the term progress. There can be no doubt about our advance in science. The trite references to the use we make of steam, of which the ancient sages knew so little as to call it smoke, establishes this beyond the possibility of denial. But, on the other hand, our advance in literature and art has been crab-like; for it has been accomplished with our face turned towards antiquity. To set up ideals out of the actualities of the past involves the recognition that we, as a race, stand lower than we have done before, or at least at one time we have slided backwards and not yet retrieved the lost ground.

The progress of humanity, with all its deviations and backslidings, may appear as one decided march onwards, if we look upon our ideals, plucked from the past, as so many pegs thrown out into the distant future demarcating the ground to be occupied by the road of civilization. The Greeks showed us, as in a flash, and within a limited space, ideals of poetry and art, and since the time of the Renaissance we have been striving to attain them. Christ has been the moral ideal held up to us for well-nigh nineteen hundred years; but this we are so far from having realized, as to be filled with doubt whether, in our awkward groping, with our faces turned towards Calvary, we move in the right direction.

There are many circumstances which render it difficult to decide whether we have progressed or not. How are we to determine which represents the greater advance, the high degree of æsthetic civilization in the small group of the human family, and all the rest plunged in barbarian darkness; or, a lower degree of æsthetic civilization uniformly spread among all the peoples of the world? We have, thus, to consider not only the degrees of progress, but the nature—whether æsthetic or moral—and its extension, before we can decide whether we have progressed or not. But this is not all. We must agree, or at least have clearly determined in our own minds, towards what goal the progression is supposed to move. If it be to bring the whole of humanity up to an ideal beauty, perfect health, and a maximum of strength and agility, our civilization in our present stage certainly tends in the other direction. If, on the other hand, the goal be the conquest of Nature's forces, we are certainly moving rapidly towards it.

In face, then, of the complexity of the question, whether humanity is progressing or not, the best method of replying to it rationally is to take one feature of human development only, but one in which the others are included, or on which they depend. To select for such a test-feature the psychological conditions of civilized humanity, at a certain period as manifested in literature and art, might at the first glance appear as the most rational course, because with strong and sound minds, with well-balanced psychological faculties, a nation is most likely to shape its destiny in such a fashion as to secure excellency in all the domains of its existence.

But there are strong objections to this method of gauging human progress. The fashionable writers and artists may not represent the mass of their contemporaries, but may be the exponents of a temporary mood in a small uninfluential clique. Features of literature and art may, as we have already pointed out, convey the impression of retrogression simply because they reflect the unrest and confusion which prevail in the majority of minds at periods when new ideas and new views, healthy in themselves, trample out the old ones. Art and literature do not always reflect the ethics of a nation at a given period. The nation may be intellectually strong and morally sound, but political events, economic troubles, may momentarily goad it into abnormal moods and drive it, by sheer necessity, into a course which, under normal circumstances, it would shun. A despot with æsthetic leanings, and his nobility, might be instrumental in causing art and literature to blossom forth most vigorously, while the people at large might be sunk in the deepest depths of demoralization and misery in order to furnish the means for the maintenance of a brilliant court. History and actualities afford ample confirmation of the fact that art and literature may flourish while the people degenerates. When the culture of Greece was in its zenith, a large proportion of the people—the slaves—had fallen so low as to afford actually object lessons to the young citizens, in order to deter them from the horrors of vice and degradation. During the Renaissance in Italy the courts were corrupt, and the Church had sunk to its deepest stage of demoralization. While the " Roi Soleil," was developing literature and art in the hot-house of his royal patronage, the immorality of the nobles and the degradation of the people were unprecedented.

Nor are there wanting examples of how a nation may be in a vigorous state of progression, without developing any remarkable features in art and literature. Switzerland was for a long time the leading nation in Europe in the matter of government, legislation, administration, civic virtues, and education, but has never distinguished itself æsthetically. During the period in which America was most progressive, its people were too busy with practical affairs to give much attention to the arts. If, therefore, we were to judge the progress of a nation by its art and literature, we might feel disposed to conclude that these two blossoms of civilization sprout forth in the same ratio as the people degenerate. But this would be absurd, for it would be to give the palm of civilization to the Esquimaux, or to the pigmies in the dark forests of Africa. The idea, therefore, of judging whether a nation, or a race, is rising or degenerating by the state of its arts, must be rejected as utterly misleading.

The political and social institutions of a nation are surely the features that best lend themselves to the test of the stage it has attained in progressive development, or degeneration. If laws and institutions are such as to give every inhabitant the best chances of attaining to a high degree of civilization, of morality, and of happiness, and such laws and institutions emanate from the people themselves, and are not imposed by another nation and not by the freak of a despot, that nation is in a progressive state. It is difficult to imagine a country with good laws and good institutions without corresponding healthy conditions in all the other features of its existence. History offers no example of a community, or of a people, that has given itself laws and institutions equally beneficial to all the individuals, and yet exhibiting signs of decay in any domain of its culture. It is true that in a free, healthy, progressive State, especially a thoroughly democratic one, literature and art may not attain that hectic florescence so often co-existent with bad laws and bad institutions. But it has never been found that art and literature in such healthy nations are in a degenerating state.

It is true that different minds hold different opinions as to the attributes of good laws and institutions. A man who believes that human beings are essentially wicked and brutal would call a government good only when it possessed power enough to keep the people in subjection; while he who has discovered that the good qualities in human beings spring from a natural instinct, and the bad ones from unfavourable conditions and corrupt surroundings, would only call that form of government good which afforded to each individual the greatest possible liberty consistent with the same degree of liberty in others. But there can be no hesitation as to what constitutes good government and good institutions, if we appeal to the only authority capable of judging with full knowledge of the case, namely, the individuals themselves.

We often meet with people who look with distrust upon institutions and systems of government based on liberty, but this does not affect our assertion that the great mass of individuals would personally, and for themselves, claim as much liberty as they could obtain. Those who advocate authoritative administration and the subjection of the people to a class, or an elected body, behold in such constitutions the means not of reducing their own liberty, but of extending it beyond legitimate boundaries, and at the expense of the liberty of others.

It is hardly possible to imagine a nation that has given itself, and is living under a system of personal liberty, and is at the same time degenerate. A degenerate man fears liberty, he prefers to lean on others; he feels not ashamed to live on charity, and would abuse his liberty in order to satisfy his base instincts. A sound-minded and morally healthy man needs no compulsion to respect the rights and liberties of others. He trusts and respects others, because he trusts and respects himself. He would assist no man in his attempts and intrigues to injure others. He would, therefore, uphold his own, as well as the liberty of others.

Such bad results as Max Nordau fears from institutions based on liberty can only arise out of oppression. We have shown how the Anti-Semitic movement, which he erroneously regards as an outcome of too much liberty, is the result of oppression exercised by the Jewish capitalists and employers in virtue of bad legislation, and no one will deny that the Anarchistic tendencies spring from the same cause. From these reasons we may fairly conclude that, if we wish to form an opinion of the intellectual soundness and moral strength of a nation, we cannot do better than examine to what an extent it has attained to good institutions based on personal liberty.

If civilized mankind is actually degenerating, we must find a tendency among the people in the countries under examination to give themselves, or to accept under compulsion, laws and institutions which rob them of their personal liberty.

In gauging the present epoch by this standard, we might first be inclined to side with Max Nordau. Those great nations which may fairly be looked upon as the leaders of civilization present spectacles of political corruption and retrogression, which might well suggest the idea that, instead of developing into a race intellectually and morally strong enough tó live free, they show a marked willingness to place themselves under control of some kind— to abandon their divine attributes and to assume those of domesticated animals. But a correct opinion about so important a question cannot be formed on a superficial glance. In no branch of knowledge are appearances so deceptive as in sociology. Apparently the same effects are often produced by two opposite causes, and under slightly different circumstances the same cause may produce two opposite effects. Thus, a man may vote for a measure because he is corrupt and selfish, and with the object of benefiting himself at the expense of his fellow men ; while another man may vote for the same measure because he does not happen to be in possession of certain special knowledge which would enable him to understand the nugatory character of his action.

There are nations in Europe at this moment presenting such a mass of anomalies as to render it extremely difficult to decide whether they are bent on improving their laws and institutions, or on making them worse. Much, for example, that has happened in Germany has been pronounced as a decided forward movement. The German army has displayed physical and mental qualities which bear witness to healthy development rather than degeneration. The unification of the German States into one Empire had for some time before the last war been the goal towards which the nation aspired. When it was reached, patriotic Germans expected it to be made the starting-point of a new departure for further progress. But the very accomplishment of national unification involved features which clearly pointed to retrogression. The mediæval principle of conquest was revised. The future peace and good-will among the nations was destroyed by the annexation of the two provinces conquered from France. Standing armies for Germany became more than ever necessary, and the nation was called upon to make enormous sacrifices in order to ward off the consequences of retrogression in foreign politics. The heaviest burdens were laid upon the working-class, and their struggle for existence became desperate. They have shown many signs of discontent, and these have led to the consolidation of repressive measures. Thus Germany now presents the spectacle of a curious amalgam of mediæval and modern features.

At the head of this great empire we find a young Emperor who, though not a despot in the widest sense of the word, possesses, as an indispensable feature of the system, sufficient power to plunge not only the whole of Germany, but all Europe, into unspeakable misery. The individuals of the nation sink into insignificance before him. They plainly feel that their destiny is in his hands as much as that of their ancestors was in the hands of their mediæval emperors. And yet the people are highly civilized, well educated, and show, in their different walks of life, intelligence, strength of character, moral worth.

Here, then, is a people, which, judged collectively by our standard, would stand at a low point of development, because their laws and institutions are not based on personal liberty. If we consider the direction in which they are moving, the verdict becomes as unfavourable. The country is torn by two divergent tendencies, neither of them aiming onwards. The one represented by the Emperor, the official bodies, the plutocrats, and men who think as Max Nordau, who wish to keep a keener watch on the destitute classes; the other represented by the socialists, who clamour for the destruction of the present system, not for the purpose of securing personal liberty, but of wresting what little is left of it from the people, and of establishing complete State tyranny.

If the standard we are applying be trustworthy, neither of the two currents of development, noticeable in Germany, run in the direction of a high degree of civilization. At the present moment it seems difficult to discover whence, within Germany, could come the impulse for such general mental and moral progress as would be manifested by good and free institutions. If the present conditions could prevail indefinitely, and gradually improve so as to safeguard, or at least not impede, the development of the individuals, Germany might look forward to the future with equanimity.

But, unfortunately, actualities in that country confirm only too well the trustworthiness of our standard. The result of the present system cannot fail to exercise degenerating effects on the people, but whether these effects will influence the present generation only, or by heredity be perpetuated in the nervous systems and the brains of the race, is a question for psychologists to settle, The stupendous standing army, the heavy taxation, and a host of bad laws, have undermined, and are still undermining, the welfare of the people. The immediate results are, among the working-classes: extreme penury, hopeless lives, low morals, intense hatred of the wealthy class, a growing sympathy with the destructive programme of the advanced anarchists, decay of religious belief without any growth of the religion of humanity of science. Among the commercial class, the results are: intense competition, small profits, nervous application to business, a thirst for gold and recklessness with regard to the means of satisfying it. Among the bureaucratic classes the dread of reduced and retarded advancement has caused discipline and absolute submission to take the place of religion and philosophy. The landed aristocracy, seeing their incomes threatened by the deplorable state of agriculture, plot and plan how to recoup themselves at the expense of the people, and have even shown an inclination to resist the Emperor himself when their interests require it. This state of affairs is more than sufficient to account for such signs of degeneration as Max Nordau has noticed in his own country. What wonder that artists and writers, menaced by misery and actuated by the general thirst for gold, should consult their market rather than their inspiration, and that they should copy successful authors and artists in France and elsewhere, rather than take the trouble and the risk to do original work. A comparison between German literature of to-day, and that of decaying Rome could not fail to impart important lessons.

Everything in Germany points to a coming catastrophe. Even, if we consider only one of the directions from which the first alarm may come—that is, the Finance Department—it seems impossible that the system can last much longer. The heavy taxation unfortunately undermines its own basis, namely, the ability of the people to pay, and the much strained credit of the State is likely to collapse at the very moment it will be most needed. It is, therefore, not premature to consider what will happen in that country at about the end of this century, when the financial resources, the patience of the people, and the confidence of the army may be exhausted.

Two alternatives are possible. The crisis which seems bound to come may be a violent one, arising from below; or it may be a peaceful one, taking its origin from above. In the one case, there will be a momentary social chaos; for all the military and bureaucratic institutions, all systems, theories, prejudices, will be cast into the furnace. At what time and under what conditions Germany will emerge from the crisis will depend on the number, and the strength of mind, of those Germans who understand that good institutions based on liberty are the cardinal attributes of a sound-minded and morally strong nation.

The other case—the crisis coming from above—does not seem possible just now, because the Emperor himself would have to take the initiative. It is not likely that he would give up his power, his military tastes and pastimes, in order to render Germany a free and happy nation, living in peace with other free nations. For a sovereign to conceive such an idea would be almost supernatural, and to carry it out successfully would require the highest degree of human intelligence, because it could not be done except in harmony and in co-operation with the other European States.

From whatever direction the crisis comes, there is much in the Germans to warrant a final successful issue. We cannot believe, with Max Nordau, that such signs as we see of degeneration spring from moral and intellectual weakness. In the external circumstances, we find sufficient cause for far more demoralisation than actually exists; and the Germans, taken as individuals, show themselves to possess plenty of those mental and moral qualities which are the only possible foundations of a healthy State. They bear witness to the fact that, despite unfavourable outward circumstances, the race is not decaying; and that the present corruption and demoralisation may be decay only of one stage of human development, from which in obedience to some strong impulse a new regenerating era may arise.

In order to elucidate the apparent state of degeneration which characterises civilization at the close of this most remarkable century, as well as its causes, we have instanced Germany—the country where Max Nordau has studied and written, and where he seems to have received his most vivid impressions. The circumstances and tendencies of other countries, especially in those governed more or less on despotic principles, are akin to those in Germany. Everywhere increasing penury, discontent among the destitute classes, a rapidly growing power among the plutocrats, national indebtedness, financial corruption, the decay of all religious belief, and general demoralisation. But the similarity does not end here. In every country there are numbers of people striving and hoping to bring about a better state of things, even at the cost and sacrifice of some of the leading features of our civilization. There is a mass of evidence, including those peculiar features of modern society, on which Max Nordau has dwelt so largely, showing that a deep unrest has taken hold of humanity. The feeling is not only that we are in a wrong position, but that we are moving in a wrong direction. The general fear is not that degeneration has set in, but that, moving on the road that we do, we cannot escape it.

The most striking characteristic of our time is that in no nation do we find, on either side of the Atlantic, any distinct indication of the road which can lead us past the Slough of Despond. The moral state of the civilized world is like a nation preparing for revolt against a tyrant : gloomy, discontented, and excited men are encouraging one another with secret signs and pass-words, mustering and drilling in secret places, to be ready for action, but without any trustworthy leaders, without any plans for the future, without even any tactics for the first struggle. In some countries the cry is for leaders ; but the old faith that the situations will bring out the men seems to have been utterly falsified : for everywhere mediocrity, prejudice, and corruption, hold the helm. The cry in England and other countries is not for leaders, but for more light. We want a higher philosophy, nobler arts, a loftier literature, sounder principles of legislation, a purer religion.

No nation holds a higher responsibility than the English. Its vast possessions all over the globe, its financial and commercial supremacy, its ethical influence over all the English-speaking countries, marks it out as the standard-bearer of civilization. Nothing great can happen among us without re-echoing in the remotest corners of the earth, and any step onward taken by us will send a thrill throughout humanity. Degenerate Englishmen may still wish to meekly follow other nations, but our mission is to be the practical, energetic, daring pioneers heading the march of progress. By using its great power and influence, the British nation can render invaluable service to humanity in the present crisis. On England must therefore rest our hopes for the practical solution of the grave questions on which progress and retrogression depend. From England alone can proceed that electrifying impulse of which the bewildered nations stand in need, that they may marshal the forces and focus the goal of progress.

In our political circles, in the ranks of literature, and throughout all the strata of society, there are already unmistakable signs that the period of scepticism, selfishness, and rant will end with the century; that scientific superstition and sickly Collectivist chimeras are doomed; and that the nation is sternly entering upon the mission of leading humanity towards good laws and institutions based on liberty, and thus inaugurating a universal movement which by its glorious results shall demonstrate that the alarming symptoms of degeneration, revealed by the psychologists, are the first symptoms of regeneration.

www.ingramcontent.com/pod-product-compliance
Lightning Source LLC
Chambersburg PA
CBHW030804230426
43667CB00008B/1055